John Lennon, My Brother

John Lennon, My Brother

Julia Baird with Geoffrey Giuliano

Foreword by
Paul McCartney

Henry Holt and Company • New York

Copyright © 1988 by Julia Baird and Geoffrey Giuliano
All rights reserved, including the right to reproduce this
book or portions thereof in any form.
Published in the United States by Henry Holt and Company, Inc.,
115 West 18th Street, New York, New York 10011.

Library of Congress Cataloging-in-Publication Data
Baird, Julia.
John Lennon, my brother / by Julia Baird with Geoffrey Giuliano.
   p.   cm.
ISBN 0-8050-0793-8
1. Lennon, John, 1940– . 2. Rock musicians—Biography.
I. Giuliano, Geoffrey.   II. Title.
ML420.L38B3   1988
784.5'4'00924—dc19
[B]   87-28642
                                            CIP
                                            MN

Henry Holt books are available at special discounts
for bulk purchases for sales promotions, premiums,
fund raising, or educational use. Special editions
or book excerpts can also be created to specification.

        For details, contact:

        Special Sales Director
        Henry Holt and Company, Inc.
        115 West 18th Street
        New York, New York 10011

First American Edition
Printed in the United States of America
10 9 8 7 6 5 4 3 2 1

To my mother

JULIA BAIRD, 1988

To my mother

GEOFFREY GIULIANO
NEW YEAR'S DAY, 1988

And, of course, to John.

'When I was a boy everything was right.'

JOHN LENNON from 'SHE SAID SHE SAID'

Contents

*Four sections of photographs
follow pages 26, 52, 104, 122.*

List of Illustrations

ILLUSTRATIONS

Waylaid during the recording of *Abbey Road*‡
John leaving his Dakota apartment (Dimo Safari; photo: Michel Senegal)
Onstage with Elton John‡ (photo: Stephen Morley)
Backstage at the London Lyceum†
John, worried about the supertaxman*
Paul outside his office in Soho‡ (photo: Karen Neilson)

Foreword by Paul McCartney

Whenever I think of the times in my early Liverpool days when John and I made the occasional visit to his mother, I also remember his two young sisters, Julia and Jacqui. My relationship with them was a passing one but we always had fun and shared at least a few twinkling moments. When Julia and I met recently after a long time it was great to see that she still had that old family sparkle.

I'm glad to learn anything I can about John's past. I know for instance how incredibly loving he was towards his mother: we were both smitten by her exuberant sense of fun and not least of all her banjo playing. In time I managed to persuade John not to play banjo chords on his guitar and eventually he trained his fingers to the correct guitar positions . . .

Great days. Great memories. Let it all flood back.

Preface by Julia Baird

A rich man asked Sengai to write something for the continued prosperity of his family, so that it might be treasured from generation to generation.

Sengai obtained a large sheet of paper and wrote: 'Father dies, son dies, grandson dies.'

The rich man became very angry. 'I asked you to write something for the happiness of my family! Why do you make such a joke as this?'

'No joke is intended,' explained Sengai. 'If before you yourself die your son should die, this would grieve you greatly. If your grandson should pass away before your son, both of you would be broken-hearted. If your family, generation after generation, passes away in the order I have named, it will be the natural course of life. I call this real prosperity.'

I have a personal understanding of this Zen wisdom. Our world collapsed with the early death of our mother. Jacqui and I were just beginning to accept this when our father died. But the death of John brought chaos to the natural order and unleashed a cacophony of feelings: rage, sadness, grief, pain, desperation. Looking back into our childhood and recalling happy days when our parents were alive makes it easier to accept. It's looking back into normality – for us, that is!

I have written this book for my mother, for her memory: a demonstration of our love for her and a reminder of hers for us. For John, to link him with his family. For my children, so that they may understand a little more. And for myself, so that I may understand too.

It tells the story of my brother John and the legend John; where he meets his family and sometimes where he doesn't. Our time together was short and cut short. This is an account of some of it.

John Lennon, My Brother

Chapter One

MEMORIES OF MUMMY

'It's very important to me for people to know that I actually had a mother. She just happened to have a husband who ran away to sea when the war was on and so she had it very rough for a while. I wasn't an orphan by any means though. My mum was very much alive and well and living only a fifteen-minute walk from my aunties'. I always saw her off and on. I just didn't live with her full time, that's all.'

JOHN LENNON

'It's really very difficult for me to listen to John's song, 'Julia', beautiful as it is. After all, she was my mother too.'

JULIA BAIRD

'As a boy John was always happy as a lark. Very whimsical, often dancing up and down, exceedingly good with us girls. Really just a big brother hanging around the house strumming on his old guitar making up little tunes and things. We were all very good friends.'

JACQUI DYKINS

I was in a shop in Penny Lane in Liverpool recently, buying a birthday card for uncle Norman – he still lives in the house John bought for him and my aunt Harrie. The lady behind the counter peered at me. 'I remember you,' she said. Then she lowered her voice to a conspiratorial whisper. 'You're John Lennon's sister, aren't you? You're Julia.' Even all these years later, I am often remembered in this part of Liverpool where John and I grew up. You would think that, by now, people would have forgotten other members of the family like me, an ordinary working mother. But the extraordinary impact that John's life and music had on so many people has meant that, even a quarter of a century after the Beatles' monumental rise to fame, I am still recognised as the sister of a world celebrity.

We didn't suddenly become aware we had a famous brother. To us, John's fame happened gradually, like his getting taller. Outsiders only remember the highlights, the so-called overnight success. It's like the aunt who suddenly arrives on the scene and proclaims, 'My goodness! Haven't you grown?' For people who are close the day-to-day changes are too fused to have any immediate effect on the consciousness.

My sister Jacqui and I were aware of John only as the clever big brother we had always known. We were just as thrilled with his first public performance on the back of a coal lorry in a Liverpool side street as we were with the Beatles' first Royal Command Performance. His emergence as the man the rest of the world knew was so gradual that we were never shocked into thinking, 'We've got a superstar in the family.'

Many people still remember Jacqui and me as John's sisters and mostly in a kind manner. That wasn't always the case for John, of course. I felt very upset for him when I read stories about him in the papers which were both ridiculously untrue and extremely hurtful. John used to shrug it off. 'It's daft, Ju,' he told me. 'But it's something you have to get used to. What's it matter? If that's what they want to write about me, let 'em.' Sometimes he got his own back and said things he didn't mean, just as a joke. Once he was reported as saying he regarded himself as a working-class socialist. He certainly had a social conscience. He was interested in numerous causes. One of the reasons Apple was set up in May 1967 was, as John put it, 'to see if we can create things and sell them without charging three times our price.' But a socialist, a millionaire like him? And a working-class lad from the slums of Liddypool, as it was known in Beatlespeak? That he never was either.

Our mother Julia came from a fairly well-to-do middle-class family. She and her four sisters were brought up in what was then one of Liverpool's smartest residential areas, in the shadow of the great red sandstone Anglican cathedral. My mother must have watched the cathedral grow. It was in the process of being built when she was born on 12 March 1914, five months before the outbreak of World War I. Liverpool was a thriving city then. With its seven miles of docks it was one of the busiest ports in the world. It was home to the Cunard Steamship Company and the world's first ocean-going liners. The docks were never empty, with a constant flow of cargo ships carrying grain and cotton from America and sugar from the West Indies.

My maternal grandparents, George and Annie Stanley, and their five daughters shared in that prosperity. Pop, as we called our grandfather, was born in 1874. He had spent many years at sea, and was now an insurance investigator working for the Liverpool Salvage Company. They lived in Huskisson Street, a terrace of fine Georgian houses on four storeys with basements for the servants. Many of the houses had pillared entrances to the front doors and ornate wrought iron balconies overlooking the street which was lit by gas lamps. The gas lamps have become electric now and the old grandeur has all but disappeared.

These lovely old houses were neglected for many years but now the Canning Development Project is undertaking complete renovation of the area. The exteriors are all being painted and the elegant interiors where the wealthy cotton merchants brought up their families and where our mother spent part of her childhood have been converted into roomy Housing Association flats.

Pop was straight-laced, kind but firm. He had all the hallmarks of the classic Victorian father, for that is how he himself had been brought up. It was learn your schoolwork, mind your manners, best frocks on Sunday with church in the morning and Sunday School in the afternoon. But his strictness was always tempered by a great warmth and affection for my mother and John at least.

George and Annie's first two children, a boy and a girl, both succumbed to fatal illnesses before their third birthday. Infant mortalities were a sad but familiar fact of life before the advent of modern medicine. Then came five healthy girls all in a row between 1906 and 1916. Mary Elizabeth (always known as Mimi) was the eldest. After her came Elizabeth (later nicknamed Mater), Ann Georgina (nicknamed Nanny), our mother Julia (sometimes called Judy), and the spoiled baby of the family, Harriet (otherwise Harrie). Our family was always very keen on nicknames. John was often called Stinker, right up until he was about twelve.

Despite their conservative upbringing, or perhaps because of it, they matured into a remarkable quintet way ahead of their time.

They were individual and determined to an extent rare among that generation of women. They were certainly never conventional, least of all Julia.

The first shock was Mimi. Girls pre-war were expected to have a family when they got married. Babies were what marriage was for. Not Mimi. She'd had enough of looking after small children with her own younger sisters. She put her foot down the minute she and George got married. 'I am not going to have any children,' she announced. And she didn't.

Nanny was a career woman, which was highly unusual in 1930. She was a civil servant and didn't marry until her mid-thirties. She had a son, Michael. As soon as he was born, she made her declaration. 'That's it. No more babies for me.'

Harrie caused a furore by going off to Cairo as the bride of an Egyptian, a student at Liverpool University. When Ali died suddenly after a tooth-extraction in Egypt, Harrie brought her baby daughter Leila back to war-torn Liverpool – with Ali's parents hot on her tracks, thwarted because they wanted custody of their granddaughter. That was dramatic enough. Then, much to the family's horror Harriet, as the widow of a foreign national, was pronounced an alien. During the war she had to report to the police station every day.

Mater had her own form of protest against convention. When she became a mother, she immediately discounted 'Mummy' as her new title. Too common a name, almost every woman she knew was called that. So Elizabeth became Mater, not only to her son Stan but to the rest of the family as well. Not that Stan stayed long enough to wonder about his mother's unusual name. He was extremely small and delicate, and when he was only a few weeks old Mater decided she couldn't cope. She handed him over to our grandmother to rear until he was big enough to go to boarding school. Mater was one of the kindest people I have ever known. But when it came to looking after the person she loved best, she was frightened out of her wits. The Stanleys always were sensitive to an extreme degree.

And then there was Julia – the most unusual and unpredictable of them all. She caused more Stanley eyebrows to rise than any other member of the family. It was hardly surprising she gave birth to someone as exceptional and original as John. Music, like originality, ran through the family. John's musical background went back a long way. Julia's grandfather, William Stanley, was a solicitor's clerk who loved playing the banjo in his spare time. It was he who taught Julia to play both the banjo and the piano as a little girl. And it was she who taught John to play chords on his very first guitar.

There were also musical genes on the paternal side of John's family tree. Jack Lennon, his Dublin-born grandfather, was a professional entertainer and a musical all-rounder who could sing, dance and play the banjo. He was born in 1855 and brought up in Liverpool where his parents emigrated when he was a baby. Then he too emigrated to find his fortune in America with his Irish bride Mary Maguire. He succeeded modestly in vaudeville and became one of the founding members of the famous

Kentucky Minstrels. He retired home to Liverpool, reasonably prosperous but certainly no superstar, and in 1912, at the age of 57, helped Mary produce the son who was to become our family's greatest source of worry. He was Alfred, or 'that Alf Lennon', which is all I ever heard my aunts call him. In fact, I have never heard a good word said about him. Whatever his faults, he certainly helped mould the future for pop music and millions of Beatles fans.

Alf's mother died during the birth of her third child. When Alf was five, his father died too. Alf and his two younger brothers, Charles and Sidney, were put into the care of Liverpool's Blue-coat School, very near Penny Lane, which took in orphans. The original building still stands – a forbidding red brick Victorian mansion with turrets and a clock tower which must have frightened the life out of the little Lennons.

At 15 Alf left the orphanage to earn his living. He had a succession of dead-end jobs before finding one that really suited him, as a bellboy in Liverpool's grand Adelphi Hotel. The luxury of the surroundings and the dapper uniform with gold buttons must have greatly appealed to the flamboyant side of Alf's nature. It was only a week after leaving the orphanage that he met Julia. She was an impressionable teenager of 14 and she fell head over heels in love with him.

In an interview many years later, this is how Alf described that first meeting with my mother: 'A mate and I were in Sefton Park on our day off and he was attempting to show me how to pick up girls. I had just bought myself a cigarette holder and a bowler hat and I fancied my chances. We had our eyes on this girl. As we walked past, she called out to me, "You look silly." So I replied, "And you look lovely", and sat down beside her on the park bench. She said that if I did want to sit next to her I'd have to take off what she called "that silly hat". I got up and threw it in the lake.'

All very romantic, but not the sort of haphazard union my grandparents envisaged for one of their daughters. Mimi says, 'He was really quite good-looking, I have to admit. But we all knew he wouldn't be any good to anyone, least of all Julia.'

In those class-conscious times, there was a social order with

7

pluses and minuses for certain jobs, the way you spoke, the house you lived in, your family background and the amount of money you had. Alf was very short on pluses.

He was a most unsuitable suitor in every way. But Julia was very headstrong. When they married at Liverpool's Mount Pleasant Register Office on 3 December 1938, not one of the Stanleys attended the wedding. Alf claimed that marriage was all Julia's idea. 'One day she said to me, "Let's go and get married." I replied that if we were going to, then we had to do it properly. She said, "I bet you won't." So damned if I didn't, just for a joke. It was all a big laugh really, getting married.'

They spent their honeymoon at the cinema. Julia was always a cinema buff, especially since the talkies had come in. She spent a great deal of time at the pictures, so, as a joke, had put 'cinema usherette' on her wedding certificate. Afterwards she went back to her parents' house in Huskisson Street and Alf went back to his rented room. The next day he packed up his meagre worldly belongings, signed on for three months and sailed off to the West Indies as a steward aboard a luxury liner. My poor mother! She was a grass widow within 24 hours, living at home with parents who were less than pleased with this madcap daughter of theirs. Alf breezed back into her life now and then, moving in with the Stanleys for a week or two at a time with no mention of any plans for a married home of his own.

After one such visit, the Christmas after the outbreak of war, Julia found that she was pregnant. Typically, Alf wasn't around to celebrate when the good news was confirmed or when she checked in to the Oxford Street Maternity Hospital the following October for the birth. It was 1940 and the Blitz was in full swing. Liverpool was suffering extremely heavy bombing. An air raid was at its height when John Winston Lennon was born at seven o'clock on the morning of 9 October. The name Winston was my mother's patriotic gesture. The new baby was immediately tucked into a cot and placed beneath her iron bedstead. It was the safest place, given the possibility of falling debris from a direct hit or flying glass from windows shattered by bomb blast. They went back home to Julia's father, Pop, now a widower and living in a smaller house in Newcastle Road. The house was in the Penny Lane area, almost opposite the orphanage where Alf had been brought up.

John had just learned to walk when Julia heard some shocking news. She had gone, as she normally did, to the shipping office to collect her money from Alf's wages. There she discovered that Alf had disappeared. He had jumped ship in America. She must have been terribly hurt. Effectively it was the end of their ten-year relationship.

Alf reappeared intermittently with various excuses – and took off again. Apparently there were odd phone calls from Southampton when his ship docked. He either hadn't got leave or, if he had, he didn't care to use it up making the journey north to Liverpool. By then Julia had had enough of her on-off marriage. She was young and fun and full of life and she obviously wanted more from a husband than Alf had to offer. Besides, John was virtually fatherless, as indeed many children were during the war. Unlike them, John never had the promise 'when Daddy comes home'. Julia was never sure of anything about Alf. His inability to commit himself was doubtless influenced by his emotionally deprived upbringing. Looking back, it seems a genuine excuse for his extraordinary behaviour. But excuses didn't much help my mother's lot then. Their marriage, as Alf himself said, was a big laugh really.

What happened next was unsurprising. Towards the end of 1944 she met a young soldier home on leave and they had a brief love affair. He disappeared from her life, went back to the front and was never heard of again. No one except my mother ever knew who he was. Again, she was pregnant.

She and John were still living at home with Pop. She was still very much the daughter of the house, even at thirty years old. Pop took charge of the situation and said it would be best for everyone if the baby was adopted as soon as it was born.

War-time pregnancies out of marriage were nothing new, but attitudes were less than tolerant towards girls who got themselves into trouble. Arrangements were made with the Salvation Army for the confinement to take place at 'Elmswood', their home in nearby North Mossley Hill Road. The adoption, too, was to be arranged by the Salvation Army.

Five weeks before the end of the war, Julia gave birth to a baby daughter she named Victoria Elizabeth. Even on the birth certificate, the father was not identified. There are only two dashes where his name and occupation should be. It is thought Victoria was adopted by a wealthy Norwegian sea captain and taken to Norway when she was only a month old. She would be in her forties now, probably with a family of her own. Does she know she is the sister of John Lennon? Does she know she still has two younger sisters living in England? Almost certainly not. Everything was hushed up by the so-discreet Stanleys. Details of her birth were only recently discovered after a lengthy check through thousands of entries in the central births register in London. Since the facts were uncovered in 1985, many people have asked why I don't try and trace her. I have no inclination whatsoever to disturb either her life or that of my own family. I only wonder how this affected my mother and how she overcame it by having Jacqui and me.

My father, John Dykins, then came into my mother's life. He was a customer at the café in Penny Lane where she did shifts as a waitress. Once again, the Stanleys were very disapproving at Julia's new choice of man. For a start she was still legally married to Alf Lennon. A divorce had never been discussed because Alf was never around to discuss anything. They also felt that my father came into the same category as Alf, 'the wrong type'. My eldest cousin Leila, the one who had come back from Egypt, was old enough by then to pick up some of the vibes of this new family hoo-ha. 'I've gathered over the years that Mimi and, to some extent, Pop had grave reservations about John Dykins' suitability as a partner for Julia. The general consensus was that this new boyfriend was rather too low class for the Stanleys and he wasn't good enough for their Julia.'

Once again Julia made up her mind and there was no stopping her. She put an end to all the arguments by taking John with her and moving in with 'Bobby', her nickname for my father. They set up home in a tiny one-bedroom flat, well away from the rest of the family in the Gateacre district.

Mimi, as the eldest, was always the family spokeswoman. After her mother died she had become the matriarch. As in many other country families, the women were the backbone of our family. They took all the decisions.

Mimi and her sisters were aghast when Julia went to live with John Dykins. Characteristically Mimi took it upon herself to intervene on behalf of my brother's best interests. Shortly after they had settled into the new flat, Mimi took the bus over one weekend – the first Stanley to visit the love nest – and demanded that John be handed over to her as Julia was no longer a fit mother.

She cited Julia's 'indiscretion' involving Victoria, plus the fact that Julia already had one husband, albeit an absent one. I am sure she was acting out of the very best motives and really did have John's interests at heart. Bobby was very firm. John was Julia's child, he said. He was hers to keep, not Mimi's. Mimi was given a short, sharp send-off.

Before long Mimi was back. This time with a young social worker. 'They are not properly married,' announced Mimi. 'John should come and live with me, at least until Julia gets her life sorted out.' The social worker must have been very embarrassed as she took in the scene. The little flat was clean and tidy. John appeared to be a happy and normal five-year-old. Julia and her unofficial husband seemed happy together. 'I am afraid that doesn't really make any difference as far as we are concerned, Mrs Smith,' she said. 'The boy, after all, is *her* son.'

How thrilled Julia must have been to have the law on her side in this decidedly unpleasant family feud. Her victory was short lived. A further inspection by the Liverpool Social Services department revealed that John didn't have his own bedroom, not even his own bed. Mummy being Mummy, she naturally just tucked him in beside her each night in their large double bed. She was told John would have to be moved away until they could find a larger flat. She had no choice. John went to live with Mimi for the time being. That's how it all started, John's years with Mimi, the famous Beatles aunt all the world knew. How ironic that Mimi, the one who vowed not to have children, should end up caring for her sister's son. It was an indication of her commitment to her responsibilities as eldest sister. She felt it was her duty to see that all the siblings had a happy childhood and she believed John was in danger of not doing so.

I remember my father as a cuddly man. I would describe him as dapper. I remember him wearing a large, baggy camel-hair coat and a brown trilby set at a rakish angle. He was black-haired and he had a moustache. He was keen on ballroom dancing, as was my mother. Their tastes were Latin American, especially the tango and the rhumba. He had a funny little nervous cough which often prompted John to refer to him as 'Twitchy' to his friends. Never to his face. He actually called him Bobby as our mother did.

'Twitchy' was only John's joke. They always got on well. People who have said they were at loggerheads are totally wrong. When John came home to us at weekends he always got pocket money from my father. When John wanted a Saturday job, it was Bobby who found a slot for him in the hotel he managed. He always made sure the tips got pushed John's way, as he did for me later when I was old enough to work. I shall always respect Bobby for not trying to cash in later on John's success, unlike his real father.

Alf Lennon was never slow in coming forward, when it suited him. John had just moved in with Mimi when somehow Alf got wind of the new arrangement after he was demobbed at Southampton. He rang up Mimi and asked to speak to John. Would he like to come on a holiday to the seaside with his daddy? Of course he said 'Yes'. Mimi agreed with the plan and the two of them set off for Blackpool.

When Julia heard that Alf had gone off with John she feared the worst. Alf admitted later it was his intention never to take John back. Julia went after them and with the help of one of Alf's old shipmates tracked them down to a boarding house on Blackpool seafront.

This is what happened then, according to Alf.

'Julia said she had come to take John away from me. She was looking for a new place, she said, and intended having John back with her. I told her I had got used to John during our little holiday and I was taking him to New Zealand with me. I asked her to come with us, so we could have another go at being a family.

'She wouldn't have any of it. All she wanted was the boy. "Let's ask *him*," I said. "It's his life." So I shout for John and he runs out, jumps on my knee and asks me if his mummy is coming back to

12

stay. No, I say, he has to decide whether he wants to live with me or with her. Without a moment's hesitation, he says me. Julia asks him once more. Again he replies, "Daddy."

'She got a bit weepy then and turned to go. John suddenly jumped up and ran to her. I never saw or heard of him again until I discovered he was a pop star.'

In Liverpool John went back to Mimi and there he stayed. The Blackpool tug-of-love must have been a shattering experience for a five-year-old. Mimi became more determined than ever before that the best thing for John was for him to live with her and uncle George. They had a comfortable house with a big garden on Menlove Avenue in the fashionable district of Woolton. The Mayor of Liverpool lived next door at one time. Mimi's house was called 'Mendips' and was always referred to as such.

We cousins were always in and out of each other's houses. I remember going to play at Mendips, romping around in the back garden and having picnic teas out there in the summer. John's room was over the front door porch where he and Paul later practised their guitars together. The porch was only small and enclosed by glass which made it a good makeshift studio with the right acoustical effects. It was also less trying on Mimi's ears when they went outside. John's room was a real boy's room, as untidy as the rest of the house was immaculately neat. Books were everywhere. Mimi was a bookworm and encouraged John to read. Over his bed was a collection of cut-out skeletons and various monsters he had made.

We had great fun pulling the string he had tied to the bed post which made them jiggle up and down in a crazy dance. John had a wild imagination from the beginning. When he was only seven he started writing his own little books which Mimi still has. *Sport, Speed and Illustrated* by J. W. Lennon was one of his first. He stuck in pictures of footballers and film stars cut out from magazines, drew little cartoons and wrote in schoolboy jokes.

Somehow Julia and Bobby never found a larger flat. Julia was very disorganised about practicalities. When she became pregnant again, they moved back in with Pop. The relationship appeared to be stable and the family became more approving. Bobby, unlike Alf, was seldom far from Julia's side. Slowly and rather reluctantly they came round to accepting Bobby as a member of the family, although there was still no talk of marriage. She was, of course, still married to Alf.

The new arrival on 5 March 1947 was me, a perfectly normal seven-and-a-half-pound baby. Shortly after my second birthday my grandfather, Pop, died and we had to move out. Pop's house was only rented and the owner put it up for sale at a price my parents couldn't afford. My mother was pregnant once more and now the Council stepped in to help.

They moved us to one of their houses on the Springwood Estate, the place that was always to be home, where John gradually began to be part of our lives. He never did become a permanent fixture. By then he had lived with Mimi for some time and had settled into school. To have moved him again would have been too unsettling.

Jacqui was born on 26 October 1949. My parents still weren't married. They never were. But the neighbours didn't know. They simply assumed that my mother was Mrs Dykins, as did all our schoolfriends. She wore two rings, which Jacqui and I were given much later. Had someone asked me, I wouldn't have known what illegitimate meant. We first found out that something wasn't quite in order the way children generally discover things – by eavesdropping.

My mother and her sisters were great ones for passing hours drinking interminable cups of tea, strong and with milk and sometimes a touch of cream. The ritual was always the same. The tea was made and then they settled down for a good long chat. They were very close. My mother's behaviour may have been regarded as 'wayward' by her sisters, but that didn't alter the deep love between them all.

One afternoon, we had been playing upstairs. Together with our cousins we crept down to the sitting room where Harrie, Mater and our mother were having one of their family discussions. Outside the door we heard one of them say something to the effect of three of them being married twice.

It didn't make sense at all. In addition to not knowing about my parents, we didn't know that Harrie had been a widow before she met Norman Birch, who was then a captain in the army. We did know about Mater because we had always heard talk of Charles Parkes, Stan's father. We never called any of them aunt which they regarded as a silly handle to someone's name. But all the uncles were called Uncle. It was a topsy-turvy family in every sense. John lived with his aunt while Stan, as a little boy, had lived with our grandmother. There were aunts and uncles who weren't formally related to us at all. There was Alf, whom we had never seen, and John, whom we thought was a full-blooded brother. They must have regarded our mother as married, even without the formalities, as she was definitely one of the 'three'.

Some Beatles critics later made out that John had grown up unhappy and alone, cut off from his family. That certainly wasn't the case. Our background was so mingled that we all belonged to each other's bit of the family. We were constantly in and out of each other's homes, with aunts who treated us like their own children, fussing about us as much – and telling us off as much – as our real mothers did.

We were all perfectly happy in the centre of a very close-knit family. Ours was an extended household of five sisters and seven children – Stan (Mater's only child), Leila and David (Harrie's two), Michael (Nanny's only one) and John, Jacqui and me. Our uncles didn't come into the picture much. They were shadowy figures in the background who went out to work and didn't infringe on our lives. Once, talking about his family in an interview, John said, 'There were five women who were my family. Five strong intelligent women. One of them happened to be my mother. Those women were fantastic. One day I might do a kind of *Forsyte Saga* about them. They were my first real feminist education.'

Of all the Stanley girls, my mother was the obviously pretty one. She cared about her looks and was very beauty conscious. She always wore bright red nail polish, on her feet as well as her hands. She gave herself regular oatmeal face-masks, kept her hands white with lemon juice, and took brewer's yeast pills for her complexion. Her adviser on these home-made beauty treatments was my cousin Leila, ten years older than me. She was a great health addict and wanted to be a doctor.

Leila, who is now a consultant, says: 'Julia was as pretty as a

15

picture. Five foot two tall, two tiny feet on six-inch heels, with shoulder-length auburn hair. A little petite doll walking down the street. People used to turn back for another look at her. When some cheeky boy gave her a wolf whistle, she would say, "Hmmm, not bad yourself." It was all light-hearted fun. She had heaps of personality and a great gift for words which made her very, very witty. No one had a bad word to say about her. She was lovely to everyone.

'If you ever went to Julia's in a bad mood, she would have you rolling about in stitches in no time. She was a thoroughly charming person. She could always capture anyone's heart.'

I remember as a little girl watching my mother as she stood in front of the mirror, brushing back her thick mop of auburn hair, getting ready for an evening out with my father. She was invariably dressed in her best and only evening dress, a fluffy pink net creation trimmed with gold and silver stars. Those nights out were rare events. My father generally worked late, caught up with the evening functions at the hotel where he started as head waiter and became manager.

Ours was a happy home. We never came home from school to an empty house. She would not have let us be latchkey children. She was always there, singing away to herself in the kitchen much of the time. She was a good cook – many soups, stews, roasts, but nothing too fancy. She seemed to get the chores over and done with as quickly as possible. My mother never wasted time on the unnecessary things of life. Housework was only a necessity if no other solution could be found. It was like that with the washing. She never had a washing machine. When my father offered to buy her one, her reply was, 'What's wrong with the laundry?' That prompted her to advise me, even though I was only ten years old at the time, 'Don't ever get a washing machine, lovey. It'll just mean hard unending work. Always use the Chinese laundry.' Washing, ironing and starching the dress shirts and stiff collars my father needed for his hotel job was not her idea of a life usefully spent.

When she read stories to us, her nose was right on top of the book. She was abysmally short-sighted. Both John and I inherited that from her. She was totally against the idea of glasses. Nanny

16

told me that Mummy threw her own in the dustbin the day she left school. My father often read her the newspapers because she could not manage the small print for too long.

When the school doctor prescribed glasses for me, she told me, 'Oh no, you don't want to wear glasses, lovey. You'll be all right.' She also told me that the most beautiful eyes could never see. Hers certainly couldn't! John always took off his glasses to play when he first started doing local gigs. It wasn't considered trendy to wear spectacles. Later of course he could afford contact lenses and it was he who encouraged me to wear them too. 'They're great,' he told me. Now I mostly wear my granny specs. When you get happier with yourself, it is easier to wear glasses. John also found that out. In the last years he, too, went back to wearing glasses. He couldn't tolerate strong lights on stage.

My father was a committed homebody, a completely different man to the nomadic Alf. He enjoyed messing about in the kitchen, up to his arms in flour, baking a supply of our favourite apple pies and sticky cinnamon buns. He was a great one for gadgets. We were the first ones in the street to have a car and, most wondrous of all, a television. He was terribly excited when we had a telephone installed. He rushed off down the road to the public call box and rang up my mother, just to check that ours actually worked.

Generally, it was a harmonious household. But sometimes the sparks flew. Both my parents were strong-willed, passionate people who had no room in their lives for grey areas. It was either all black or all white with them. When they disagreed, we all knew about it. But the next minute they were kissing and making up. There was lots of affection in our house. We were quite used to walking into the room to find my father standing with my mother cuddled in his arms.

Outsiders must have thought John's live-in arrangement with his mother's sister was most peculiar. Of course it was an odd set-up; it just took me years to realise it. As a little girl, I didn't think it too strange that my big brother lived with my aunt. We certainly weren't the only family in our street with odd domestic arrangements. There was one family with nine children, two of whom lived with their grandmother – the house wasn't big enough for them all. The children in another family were looked after by their father because their mother only came home at weekends – he was out of work but she had managed to find a job 200 miles away in London.

John never spoke about his father. If he had, we would not have known what he was talking about. We assumed we all shared the same Daddy. We had never been told otherwise. It didn't strike us as odd that John called Daddy by his nickname, Bobby. Older brothers were allowed to do a variety of things which we weren't. Besides, they both had the same Christian names, like other fathers and sons we knew. Even though John's surname was different to mine, it somehow never occurred to me that we had different fathers.

We were well into our teens before we finally unravelled the complexities for ourselves. We were never *told* anything. The children in the Stanley family were always protected from any truth which the adults thought unpalatable. It was a hangover from Pop's Victorian upbringing. As children, our world was entirely separate from the world the grown-ups lived in. Nothing untoward happened in ours, apart from an occasional smack.

We always came first, had the best of everything. How could we be happy if we were weighed down with the adults' dramas and problems? We were protected from reality in every sense. Today I sit down and talk things over with my children. We never had such family discussions. John, like us, accepted the state of affairs. Alf was a distant memory. As he said later, 'I soon forgot my father. But I saw my mother frequently and I often thought about her. Distances don't mean much when you are small. I didn't realise for a long time she lived only a couple of miles away. When I got older, big enough to go on the bus on my own, I saw her all the time. She became a sort of young aunt or big sister to me. When I started having the usual teenage rows with Mimi, I used to go and live with my mother for the weekend. She gave me my first coloured shirt. She was aware of things like fashion, years before it was cool.'

My room had a double bed. When John came to stay, Jacqui moved in to sleep with me and John had her room. My first concrete memory of him is hearing him tip-toeing into Jacqui's smaller bedroom on Friday nights, long after we two were supposed to be fast asleep. In the morning we couldn't wait to rush in and jump all over him, shrieking with delight as he tickled us silly. Finally, he would shout out, 'Mummy, come and get these girls off me will you please?' That was her cue to run in and shoo us away. 'Come along girls,' she used to say. 'John wants to get dressed.'

With my father working late, she and John sat up together after we were in bed chatting and listening to records. She was an ardent Elvis fan from the very beginning, and we grew up on a diet of his records, amongst others. Mummy liked him to such an extent that when we got a kitten (at my insistence) it was christened Elvis. The cat later produced a litter of kittens in the bottom of the kitchen cupboard – so we realised our mistake – but the name remained the same!

Sometimes we saw Mummy and John as they jived around the lounge to Elvis hits. 'Hound Dog', 'Heartbreak Hotel', 'Jail House Rock' and 'Teddy Bear' were always played. When our cousin Leila stayed she would also join in. Despite the three years between them, she and John got on exceptionally well. They and Stan, Mater's son, were the eldest cousins and they usually spent the school holidays together in Scotland. At the end of term Stan joined them from boarding school and the three of them took the bus to Edinburgh where Bert, Stan's stepfather, was a dentist.

'We loved going to Mater's,' says Leila. 'She was so good natured and easy going with us children. John was a very sweet and gentle person, too. He and I often had quite serious talks together. We discussed the rights and wrongs of the world and what we would do with our lives. I loved being with Julia as much. She was such great company. She was mad about all her children but I know she held a very special place in her heart for John. After all, he was her first child and her only son.'

My mother never showed any favouritism. Sometimes, she sat me on her knee and listened over and over again to a record called 'My Son John', sung by a baritone with the deepest voice. But my sister and I never felt left out.

I remember her holding me up beside her, my cheek pressed next to hers, looking at us together in the mirror and saying, 'Oh, I *do* love you.' She was uninhibited in her affections.

She loved actively playing with us. For Julia, playing was a serious business. Her favourite game was turning the kitchen into a Co-op so that we could play shops. She was always the nice lady behind the counter. 'Good morning, Madam,' she would say to me and my friends who were being the customers. 'Can I help you?' John, disguised with a black paper moustache, took the part of the cashier. The real Co-op shops in those days had an overhead wire with a shuttle which carried the change between the counter and the cash till. My mother compromised with our indoor clothes line, a rope pulley system with wooden slats to hang the clothes on so they could be hoisted up to the ceiling to dry. She placed the money for our 'purchases' in a small tin cup, secured it to the rope, and sent it whirling over the kitchen to John. When he sent back the 'change', she would tell him in a mock posh voice, 'Madam says you have shortchanged her.' John would reply every bit as poshly, playing along with the make believe for his little sisters. 'Just you tell Madam from me, she can't count!' One evening as my father opened the kitchen door in the middle of the Co-op game, the clothes line came crashing down on his head. For at least two seconds he was out cold while my mother laughed her head off.

One of our special outings was going off to see Nanny who lived 'over the water', which in Liverpool means across the Mersey River in Cheshire. To get there, we had to take the train through the famous three-mile Mersey Tunnel which was then the longest underwater tunnel in the world. As soon as the train entered the pitch black void, Mummy and John started on one of their double acts. Jacqui and I were a pleasingly gullible audience. 'Look! Look!' John would cry out. 'Did you see that mermaid?' He was very much the big brother in this silly childish game. 'My goodness!' my mother would answer back. 'I could have sworn it was a shark with lipstick on.' They loved to lark about like that. The zanier the game was, the better they both liked it.

John was always amusing Jacqui and me with funny little drawings which he dashed off as we watched. He had been good at art right from the beginning with his little illustrated books as a child, the cartoons he could draw in a flash, the strange

20

monsters and psychedelic paintings on his bedroom wall at Mendips. If he was there when we had homework which required an illustration, he helped us out with a picture of a terrifying dinosaur or a Roman soldier in a magnificent uniform which our teachers surely guessed we could never have done ourselves. If our schoolfriends were there, John would do their homework as well. I recently met an old schoolfriend who says that she wishes she had kept all the drawing homework John had done for her. His talent must surely have come from our mother who could draw and paint as spontaneously as he could.

When she told us stories, which she made up as she went along, she drew the characters for us on a sketch pad as the story progressed. Sometimes she painted water colours, a still-life of a bowl of apples in the kitchen or a painting of the sea when we went on holiday to Rhyl in North Wales. Once she painted a huge yellow daffodil on the bathroom wall. Underneath she wrote: 'Do you want your teeth to look like a Spring daffodil? Then don't brush them!'

She was artistic in so many ways, not least musically. 'My mother could play any stringed instrument there was,' John once said proudly. Her favourite was her mother-of-pearl banjo which had belonged to her Grandfather Stanley, who had taught her as a child how to play. She had no formal musical training after that. She always played by ear, the same as John did. She used to play and sing nursery rhymes to us, like 'Three Blind Mice' and the jokey version of 'My Son John' which went like this:

Diddle diddle dumpling my son John
Went to bed with his trousers on
One sock off and one sock on
Diddle diddle dumpling my son John

As little girls, how we loved that one. We clapped and screamed with delight, all the more if the subject of the song happened to be present. She was a fun mother, no doubt about that.

She could sing better than anyone in the family, maybe even John. And she could dance to any record you put on. She was also a great mimic and frequently had everyone in stitches when she

21

took off some local character we all knew. Juggling was another talent of hers. She could make oranges bounce through the air as rapidly as any professional juggler we had seen. She did briefly toy with the idea of singing and playing the banjo semi-professionally. She was going to have a manager and a booking agent. It wasn't to be a Broadway-style début, just entertaining at pub evenings and parties for the various local organisations. She performed a couple of times and then the idea fizzled out. She was too lighthearted to take anything beyond her family very seriously.

My father's big wind-up gramophone was the highlight of social evenings at home. That's how Jacqui, John and I first became acquainted with the strange new music from America called Rock 'n' Roll, which the local seamen had brought back with them. From the moment my mother put on an Elvis record for John to listen to for the very first time, he was a confirmed addict. It was the same when she introduced him to Buddy Holly via the gramophone.

'The very first tune I ever learned to play was "That'll Be The Day",' John told an interviewer many years later. 'My mother taught it to me on the banjo, sitting there with endless patience until I managed to work out all the chords. She was a perfectionist. She made me go through it over and over again until I had it right. I remember her slowing down the record so that I could scribble out the words. First hearing Buddy absolutely knocked me for a loop. And to think it was my own mother who was turning me on to it all.'

John's first ever musical instrument was an old mouth organ which George, Mimi's husband, had given to him. It was his most treasured possession. He took it with him everywhere, not wanting to lose sight of it for a single moment. Naturally enough, at the start of the school holidays, he took it with him when he went up to Scotland to stay with Mater.

Mimi remembers it. 'He was trying to play it on the bus all the way up,' she says. 'He must have driven the other passengers mad, I am quite sure. At any rate, the bus driver was rather taken with him. When they finally arrived in Edinburgh, he told John that if he came down to the bus station next morning he would give him a really good harmonica. John kept up everyone at Mater's half the night going on about it. In the morning he was down at the bus station first thing. He must have been about ten at the time.

'That bus driver had no idea what he started.'

John adored his uncle George and George worshipped him. In Alf's absence, John looked upon him as a father, whilst John was the son that George had never had. One Sunday afternoon in June 1955, when John was fourteen and a half, his beloved uncle suddenly collapsed and dropped dead from a liver haemorrhage. Leila, who was then sixteen, remembers clearly what happened. She says: 'No one knew George was ill. It came completely without warning. It was a terrible shock to us all, but especially to John who looked on him as a father. George was a gentle giant, six foot tall with a mound of silver hair, who often hit the door frame when he walked into a room. He was the most kind, pleasant, unaggressive man with not a cross word to say. He and John always had little secrets going on between the two of them. He was so affectionate. John always used to insist on giving him "squeakers", his name for kisses, before George put him to bed.'

Mimi is, and always was, an exacting person. But she demands the same high standards for herself. She and John invariably fell out at times over points of discipline as he began to mature. George was his good friend, the ally on his side when things weren't going too well with Mimi. That made his uncle's loss all the more considerable. He said afterwards, 'I never learned to be sad publicly, what you were supposed to say and all that. So I just went upstairs with Leila and we both had hysterics. We just laughed and laughed. I felt very guilty afterwards because I did care very much about George. Just couldn't show it, I suppose. George had always been exceptionally kind to me.'

Our uncles were always like that. They were never the domineering heads of the house who laid down the law. The Stanley girls were too strong-minded to put up with that kind of treatment. And because of their particular personalities, almost the only role for the husbands was that of provider.

Leila explains: 'The primary function of the men was to produce the money. Quite truthfully, the women were only as

23

nice to them as they had to be for the bills to be paid. There were no rows or shouting. The men just weren't very important. It was such a very large family with all the kids about needing so much attention, these men just didn't feature.'

John must have been very aware of this attitude towards the menfolk as he grew up. It may well have contributed to both his early Beatles machismo as well as the house-husband role which he adopted when his second son, Sean, was born.

Yoko discussed that point with my co-author Geoffrey Giuliano in 1982. She told him: 'John was an Englishman who was raised in a household where the primary female influence was exceptionally strong-headed, independent, yet obviously caring.

'He probably would have heard things like, "It's time to get some milk for the cats, dear," and the men would all be tending the garden. John had that side to him. Just making tea for us was a very natural thing for him to do. He had a vulnerable side to him and I had the tough side, I suppose. So we can all change roles once in a while. That was really quite natural for him and me.' As a boy, John was happiest in his role as ringleader in his circle of chums. He was daring and fearless. In almost every adventurous situation that arose, he was right there at the front. He was never afraid to stand up to his teachers, always pushing his luck right to the very edge of acceptable behaviour. If any of his friends made a dare, John was always the first to offer to take it on. He loved a challenge. In the old days he probably would have been an explorer.

Paul McCartney also grew up in Liverpool, although we didn't get to know him until he was about fourteen. It is exactly how he saw John the schoolboy.

'I think John had great wanderlust,' says Paul. 'He had an extremely adventurous streak. You could see that the way he behaved.

'He always tackled everything head on with the greatest of confidence. If he hadn't become a Beatle, I can imagine a scenario where he might have first worked as a commercial artist in his late teens. Then maybe he'd have gone off in a boat somewhere at twenty-one or two or three. You know, he did have this rather colonial attitude like a lot of the British. "We're gonna go and quell the natives and teach them a thing or two." That was John.'

Our maternal grandmother, Annie Millward Stanley, who was much loved and often talked about by her five daughters

BELOW: Leila, with her mother Harrie, my mother and Nanny in Nanny's garden, summer 1949. These women had a profound influence on all of us, throughout both our childhood and adult lives

Mimi and John with Sally, the dog

Mimi and Uncle George with John. John adored George, and was shattered by his sudden death

John's father or 'that Alf Lennon', which is all I ever heard my aunts call him

On the front porch at
Mendips

BELOW: Steadying his
bicycle for posterity

ABOVE: The children together in Nanny's garden, summer 1949. Left to right, Michael, Leila, David, Julia and John (aged 9)

ABOVE: Stanley, Leila and John on holiday with Mater in Fleetwood

RIGHT: John, outmanoeuvred by Michael in Mimi's front garden, 1950

RIGHT: Stanley and John
outside Mendips

BELOW: John and Leila with David, 1949

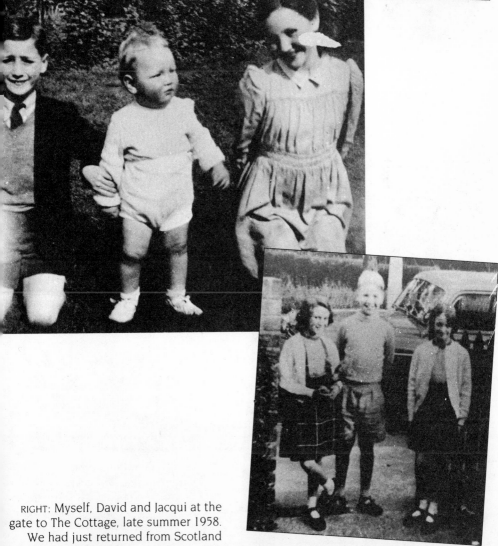

RIGHT: Myself, David and Jacqui at the
gate to The Cottage, late summer 1958.
We had just returned from Scotland

Mummy and John in Nanny's garden, summer 1949

BELOW: Mummy and Jacqui in Nanny's garden, 1950

ABOVE: Mimi and John outside Mendips. It was Mimi who cared for John on a day-to-day basis for so many years

The earliest known portrait of John

John, aged 4. Uncle Norman says of him at this age: 'John was a wonderfully intelligent little boy. He always seemed to have a grin on his face with those insightful, darting, gooseberry eyes.'

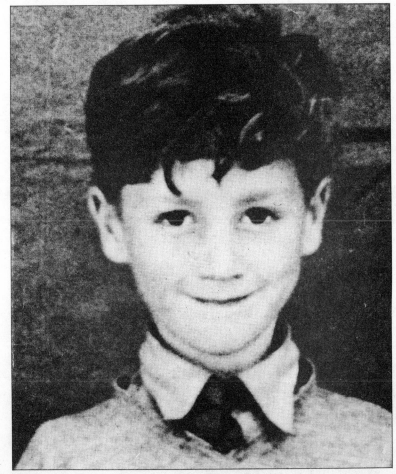

John, the mischief-maker

ABOVE: John Albert Dykins. Daddy with Jacqui in 1960, after Mummy had died

LEFT: Myself, aged 11, at school in Liverpool, 1958

Chapter Two

BATHROOM BEATLES

'They said that our love was just fun
The day that our friendship begun
There's no blue moon in history
There's never been that I can see . . .'

LENNON/MCCARTNEY, from their very first composition,
'JUST FUN'

'When I was about twelve I used to think I must be a genius,
but nobody's noticed. If there is such a thing as a genius, I
am one. And if there isn't, I don't really care.'

JOHN LENNON

Everyone talked about the May of 1956 for weeks afterwards. So did we. But not because it was the hottest May for thirty-four years and the driest for half a century. At the grown-up age of fifteen and a half, our big brother launched himself on the world of showbusiness with his very first public performance. Admittedly his stage was only a coal lorry, but for my sister Jacqui and me, six and nine at the time, it was an incredibly exciting event in our lives. We had been on a Sunday School outing that day, on a picnic to Helsby Hill, a local beauty spot. When we returned to the Church Hall our mother was waiting with some fantastic news. Instead of being hurried home to supper and bed as we expected, she was taking us to see John and his schoolboy skiffle group make their debut.

These days we never saw John without his guitar, the one our mother had bought him for £10 which was now well battered from use. A diet of Lonnie Donegan and Elvis Presley on 78s had swept him along on a tide of wild enthusiasm for Fifties' pop music. He and his friends were always round at our place playing their guitars. Somehow the noise never worried our mother. Far from it. She loved every moment of it. The louder the house throbbed to the beat of rock and roll, the better she liked it. Her musical taste included classical and jazz. It was quite different with Mimi, the aunt John lived with. She had very different musical tastes to her sister and she found rock music an intolerable noise. Besides, she felt John should be studying, swotting up for his GCE exams the following year, not playing about with guitars.

John was naturally the leader of the group. From the time he was a little boy with his own gang, he always had been the one who had to be in charge. Their instruments weren't much to talk about. Two cheap guitars, an old banjo, a washboard and a set of drums one of them had wheedled out of an uncle. At that time hundreds of other boys in Liverpool were caught up in the same musical momentum and skiffle groups were queueing up to show off their talents. John and his group finally got their big chance when they were invited to play at a street party being held by the residents of Rosebery Street to celebrate Empire Day.

John's instructions to my mother were to get off the bus at Princes Avenue. We walked nearly the whole length of the avenue and still hadn't found him, when suddenly we heard the first faint strains of that decidedly familiar sound. The noise led us there. We found John and his four friends perched up on a lorry parked across the middle of the street, playing their hearts out in a frenzy of rock and roll as the younger Rosebery residents jived around them in a swirling mass. People were hanging out of the windows of the small terraced houses, laughing and shouting, and women were standing on the doorsteps dancing to the beat of the music. We had never seen such a happening, and to think our brother was in the middle of it all!

John caught sight of us and hauled us two girls up on to the tailboard with him, whilst Mummy leaned on a nearby lamppost and watched, smiling. And there we sat open-mouthed, as Johnny and the Rainbows – as they called themselves that evening because they all wore different coloured shirts – let rip. They got no money, of course. They regarded it as a privilege to be allowed to perform.

'We didn't mind about not being paid,' John recalled later. 'We just played for fun. We were constantly changing the name of the group from some daft thing to another. I remember one night it even got changed three times before our last number.

'After Rosebery Street, we played at blokes' parties and local dances and things like that. Got a few bob if we were lucky. Sometimes it was a wedding which was always an extra good gig as it usually meant all the free beer we could guzzle and a good meal to go with it.'

My mother was the group's unofficial wardrobe mistress. She went to Garston open air market to buy the coloured shirts they wore at that gig. The Teddy Boy look was the big fashion and they wore shoestring ties and took in their trousers to make them drainpipes. If their mothers could be talked into it, they got themselves DA haircuts.

Our mother was very easy going. Besides, she was their biggest fan. I remember how proud she was that John had managed to organise such an ambitious undertaking all on his own. She never nagged him about his schoolwork, or told him he should be off to his room at Mimi's, getting down to it. Inevitably, with all the diversions, he wasn't progressing academically at all. He had been put into the C stream of his year at Quarry Bank High School. 'The dummies' class', he called it.

The one and only public exam he ever did pass in his life was the Eleven Plus for entrance into Quarry Bank, an old-fashioned boys-only grammar school where the masters aped their public school counterparts and wore black gowns. John would have much preferred the informal style of the place it is today. It has linked up with the girls' grammar next door and become a large campus-style comprehensive school.

John's two best friends were his classmate Peter Shotton and Ivan 'Ivy' Vaughan who lived near John but went to school at the Liverpool Institute. The Institute was for the bright lads. It was the best known of Liverpool's grammar schools and had a dazzling list of old boys including High Court judges, politicians, even a Nobel Prizewinner and, eventually, one of the world's best known musicians – Paul McCartney, Ivan Vaughan's school-friend.

With a grand total of eight weeks' experience behind them, John's group regarded themselves as seasoned old pros, ready for a permanent name. They chose The Quarrymen, after their school. Their first gig under the new name was on 15 June at our parish church fête in Woolton. John had been to Sunday School there as a little boy, and we still attended. It was an uneventful gig, except for one thing. Chance and luck coincided, and our brother and Paul McCartney met each other for the first time.

I went to see Paul again recently at his elegant office in London's Soho Square, not having seen him in years, and I found he had hardly changed at all. He was still the same Paul I first knew, but with a definite distinguished air about him now. I took him a packet of Everton Mints, Liverpool's famous sweets, to remind him of what was once home. He was warm and welcoming, the same friendly happy person despite the fact he is now a multi-millionaire and not the kid from the council estate he was that day at the Woolton Fête.

He remembered it sure enough. It was a landmark in the Beatles' history, the first trickle which started the stream which fed the tributary which put the river into the full flood of Beatlemania.

'At school one day Ivy Vaughan invited me along to this fête the following Saturday,' Paul told me. 'I was nearly fourteen and John was nearly sixteen. I remember coming up on the fête from across the field and hearing this great music which turned out to be from the Quarrymen's little Tannoy system.

'I was very much into music. Ivy said he knew a couple of lads in the group. "After their set, I'll introduce you," he promised. John was singing a lovely tune by the Del Vikings called "Come Go With Me". He had heard it on the radio and didn't know all the words, so he made up his own. "Come go with me down to the penitentiary", stuff like that. His guitar only had four strings and he played it like a banjo, with banjo chords, as that was all he knew. He had his glasses off and he looked very suave. Until Buddy Holly came along, fellows who wore glasses always took them off to play. After that, anyone who really needed them could come out of the closet.

'We always thought John was pretty cool. He was that bit older and he was allowed to get away with things we weren't. His hair was greased back into a drake. With that and his nice big sideboards, he did look a bit of a Ted.

'After it was over I met them in the Church Hall. We talked and then I picked up a guitar lying there and started to play "Twenty Flight Rock". I suppose I was showing off a bit. I knew all the words and they didn't. That was big currency.

'Then I did my Little Richard imitation, went through all his stuff I knew. John seemed quite impressed. There was nearly two years between us, so he was a big man in my eyes.

'Later we went down to the pub and I had to try and kid the barman I was really eighteen. Then word spread that some muscle might be needed as a gang up the street was threatening to storm the pub. I got a bit scared then. I'd just come for a nice day out and now I was with all these men who were about to lay into each other. Thankfully it all blew over and the evening turned out really good.

'A couple of weeks later Pete Shotton, John's mate, came over to my place on his bike and asked if I wanted to join The Quarrymen.

'One of the first things I realised about John when I got to know him was that he came from a very different world to my working class one. My family was from the housing estate, like the rest of the Beatles. My dad was a cotton salesman and my mum was a midwife and we lived in a council house that went with her job.

'John's relations were definitely middle-class. I remember being very impressed seeing the entire works of Winston Churchill on a bookshelf at Mendips, John's house. I was even more impressed when I learned he had actually read them.

'His people seemed to have quite a lot of money, at least by my standards. I recall him getting a hundred quid off one of his aunties for his twenty-first birthday.

'He talked about people his family knew who worked for the BBC, or his uncle who was a dentist and his aunt who lived in Scotland. It was all very exotic to me. He had apparently been all the way up to Edinburgh several times on his own by the time he was twelve. What adventure! The furthest I had been, and then always with my parents, was Skegness, almost next door to Liverpool.'

We, of course, had gone to the Woolton Fête with our mother and so had two of her sisters, our aunts, Harrie and Nanny. They were delighted with The Quarrymen. Mimi, the aunt John was closest to, had elected not to come. Not her sort of scene. She much preferred classical music and the traditional dance orchestras of the Fifties she heard on the BBC, like Victor Sylvester. Besides, she didn't want actively to encourage this new dimension to John's life, this crazy rock and roll business.

She was increasingly worried about his progress at school and his forthcoming exams. 'If you don't settle down to work soon, goodness knows what's going to become of you,' she told him. Then came the remark now known the world over: 'The guitar's all right, John, but you'll never make a living with it.'

Elvis's father had told him almost the same thing and Alan Durband, Paul's English master at the Liverpool Institute, was another one who had to eat his words. Later on, after Paul passed his A levels, he asked Alan what he should do. Go to teacher training college as he had planned? Or take up this fantastic chance to play in a club in Hamburg for £20 a week?

Says Alan: 'That was a fortune in those days. But I told Paul, "Get your qualifications. You can always play the guitar in the evening." Fortunately, he didn't take my advice.'

Mimi could be disapproving at times, not only about John's behaviour but about his friends, too. She thought some of them were a bit rough, and definitely irresponsible, and weren't any good for John.

Paul remembers her clearly. 'She was a very forthright, middle-class woman,' he told me. 'Most of the women I knew were off the estate and, quite honestly, were rather common. Mimi wasn't like that at all. I can hear her saying in her rather grand way: "John, your little friend is here to see you." The tone was rather disdainful and seemed to imply she didn't think much of you. Just as I was starting to wish I had stayed at home, I'd notice this little twinkle in her eyes which let me know she did quite like me after all.

'She had a habit of keeping people at arm's length. I had a feeling, though, she approved of me more than she did some of his other friends.

'Upstairs John was often busy writing at his typewriter in his famous *In His Own Write* style. I was very impressed. I had never known anyone before who owned a typewriter.

'We never played our guitars indoors at Mimi's house. If we didn't go round to Julia's and we stayed there, then we practised outside the front door in the glass porch. John told me Mimi banished him out there from the first day he brought home his guitar, on account of all the noise. He didn't mind, though. He liked it out on the porch as the echo of the guitars bounced nicely off the glass and the tiles.'

John's rapid rise to local fame had its effect on the schoolgirl population in our neighbourhood. As big boss of The Quarrymen, swaggering about in his Ted outfit, he was obviously a more exciting proposition than the average spotty-faced schoolboy with only a bike to his credit. His first fully-fledged fan was a strawberry blonde called Barbara. She was only a schoolgirl, but to Jacqui and me she was like a film star with lots of long, blonde hair and glamour.

She hung about outside our house for hours at a time, waiting to see John. When it first started happening, Jacqui and I couldn't make out what she was doing there. John must have suspected and our mother must have guessed, although she was much too discreet to say anything. We learned later that first she would go to Mimi's house, where John normally lived. Not finding him there, she came to our house, walking all the way to save the bus fare. John's friends always knew that was where to find him if he wasn't at home with Mimi. 'That poor girl,' my mother would often say, giving a tremendous sigh. One day Barbara was hanging around as usual, standing by the lamppost where we had set up a tarzan swing. When we went out to play, she called me over and asked me to get John to come outside.

I raced inside with the message. John only gave a deep groan and begged our mother to please go out and send her away. Just a little annoyed by all this nonsense, my mother marched out to the front gate and called out politely but firmly, 'What is it you want, dear?' At the sight of her, the poor girl took to her heels and ran off up the road.

Jacqui and I thought it was a great giggle, thoroughly enjoying the drama and Barbara's acute embarrassment. We set off after her, wanting to make the most of her discomfort, and caught up with her at the top of the road. To our amazement, instead of being further abashed by our tormenting, she turned to us like long lost friends. Please, please, she begged, run home and persuade John to come and meet her. This time John's mood had miraculously changed. Casually he strolled out of the front door and up the road for his encounter with Barbara. We followed them, waiting to hear John give her a good telling off. What happened next was totally unexpected. They embraced in a passionate kiss and sank down out of sight in the long willowy grass behind an old stone wall.

We had another terrible fit of the giggles. Sheepishly, John poked his head up over the wall and hissed at us to go away. We didn't, of course, and he had to bribe us in the end with half a crown, making us promise not to say anything to anyone.

Later that evening over dinner, our mother berated John for allowing Barbara to walk all the way from Woolton, when he didn't want to see her. Only some timely kicks in the shins under the table stopped us blurting out the remarkable truth.

Admirers seemed to be all very well if they presented themselves on a plate, otherwise John as a sixteen-year-old had little time for anything else but his music.

'Before Elvis, there was nothing,' he once said. 'It was Elvis who got me buying records. I always thought that early stuff of his was great.

'With Bill Haley, it was different. When his records came on the wireless, my mother used to like them okay. Always Radio Luxembourg or AFN, never the BBC as they didn't go in for that kind of stuff. But his records didn't do anything for me.

'I went to see *Rock Around the Clock* and I was very surprised. Nobody was screaming and nobody was dancing in the aisles like I'd read. Must have all been done before I got there. I was all set to tear up the seats, too, but nobody joined in.

'No, it was definitely Elvis who got me hooked on beat music.' When Elvis's first two films, *Love Me Tender* and *Loving You*, hit Liverpool, the Gaumont cinema put on a special double matinée. Naturally John was going to see them and he asked our mother: 'Do you want me to take the girls?'

We would have gone to see anything with John. To be taken anywhere by our important big brother was an enormous treat. What we didn't expect, though, was to be deserted halfway through the programme and left on our own. John leapt up, warned us not to move a single inch until he got back, and raced out of the cinema.

We never did discover what his urgent appointment was – probably smoking Woodbines behind the pictures. All I remember is having to sit for hours, itching to leave, having to watch a double dose of the Pathé News and the local adverts, and Elvis yet one more rollicking time. John reappeared at last and hustled us off to a park nearby for a quick spin on the roundabout and a couple of half-hearted shoves on the swings before returning us home. 'You've been out a good long time,' said our mother. 'Enjoyed yourselves?'

'Yes, Mummy,' we replied, smiling weakly. 'It was lovely.' And then we rushed outside to let off steam and recover from the longest afternoon of our lives. John was growing up and away from us. He was getting on for seventeen and two much younger sisters hadn't much place in a busy teenage life filled with his mates, his girlfriends and, most of all, his music.

'I used to have to borrow a guitar at first, before I had my own,' John said afterwards. 'My mother bought it from a mail order firm and it had a label on the inside which said, "Guaranteed not to split." I suppose it was a bit crummy, but I played it for a long time and got in a lot of good practice.

'I wanted a guitar because I had the usual kid's desire to get up on the stage. A mate of mine had one first and it fascinated me. I couldn't wait to get my own.

'My mother taught me quite a bit, my first lessons really. Most of our stuff then in the early days was just twelve bar boogies, nothing fancy.

'Of course, Paul came along later and taught me a few things. All in all, I guess I was lucky to have had the little musical training I did. I never thought of it that way at the time. All I knew I was having a helluva lot of fun.'

Paul was frequently round at our house practising with John. He and my mother got on extremely well. She had a really soft spot for him. He looked younger than he was and had this chubby little face which made him look like some angelic choirboy. He actually had been one, at St Barnabas near Penny Lane, until his voice broke. He obviously brought out my mother's maternal feelings. He was also very fond of her.

Paul told me: 'I always thought of Julia as being an exceptionally beautiful woman. She was very, very nice to us all. John just adored her, not simply because she was his mum but because she was such a high-spirited lady.

'She taught him to play the banjo and that's quite something for a mother to do. My family was musical as well, but there certainly weren't any women around who could play the banjo! That sort of activity was generally left to the men.

'She was always teaching us new tunes. I remember two in particular, "Ramona" and, oddly enough, "Wedding Bells Are Breaking Up That Old Gang Of Mine". Much later, during the Beatles years, John and I often tried to write songs with that same feeling to them. "Here, There and Everywhere" was one we wrote along those lines.

'Julia was lively and heaps of fun and way ahead of her time. Not too many blokes had mothers as progressive as she was. My own mother, being a nurse, wasn't by any means prudish, but she was a stickler for hygiene, keeping clean and all that. I rebelled against it by attempting to hang around in my dirty jeans as much as I could.

'But she loved to see us doing well and she wouldn't have really much cared how we did it. That was always one of my deepest regrets, her not being there to see the Beatles make it.'

Once John and Paul had met, the nucleus of what would finally be the Beatles was nearly complete. Only guitarist George Harrison was missing, and he wasn't so very far away. George lived near Paul and, like him, went to the Liverpool Institute. They travelled in to school together every morning on the same bus route and changed buses at the Penny Lane terminal, at the intersection of Penny Lane with Smithdown Road, the main route into the centre of the city.

The terminal was only small. It had a Ladies and a Gents, and there was a shelter place where the bus drivers sat in their break and drank cups of tea. Today the public conveniences and the drivers' snack bar have gone and the Sgt Pepper's Country Kitchen has taken over the terminal site. The owners probably don't realise just how appropriate the name of their restaurant is. One of the best known songs in the Beatles' famous *Pepper* album had its origins in those bus journeys to school.

'Everyone says that "A Day In The Life", Paul's song from *Pepper*, was about drugs,' says Institute Old Boy Steven Norris, an MP until he lost his seat in the 1987 General Election, who made the bus journey to school with them. 'Paul always claimed it was about catching the bus to school. I agree. It's exactly what we used to do. Went upstairs and had a smoke, somebody spoke and I went into a dream.'

'That's just how I remember it. Getting sleepily out of bed, dragging a comb across your head, then going out and catching the bus, upstairs to the top deck like we all did, still not properly awake, and having an untipped Woodbine.'

George was a little 'un, in the year below Paul, and looked more like twelve than fourteen. But he was music mad and that was enough, even when a school year was almost a generation gap, to make them friends out of school as well. They began spending much of their spare time together practising guitar chords until, through Paul, George joined The Quarrymen.

Paul told me: 'George was always my little mate. But he could really play the guitar, particularly a piece called "Raunchy" which we all loved.

'If anyone could do something as good as that, it was generally good enough to get them in the group.

'I knew George long before John and any of the others. They were all from Woolton, the posh district, and we hailed from the Allerton set which was more working class. George and I had got to learn the guitar together and we were chums, despite his tender years as it seemed to me then. In fact, George was only nine months younger than I was.'

My brother was fairly sceptical about admitting such a 'baby' into the group. George, his junior by only just over two years, was hardly a catch for a veteran like him. How would it look for someone as talented and popular as John to be caught consorting with an undistinguished slip of a lad like George? There were his mates to think about, never mind girls.

It must have been a big problem for him to be torn between a choice of George's talent and his own reputation. After all, the whole point of being a band in the first place was to prove you were big enough to stand on your own feet apart from your parents. And how could you do that when you had scraggy juniors like George, barely out of short pants, spoiling your image? In the end, George was too good not to include.

George's formal audition took place on the top deck of a green Liverpool bus one summer day in 1957. This, says Paul, is what happened: 'George slipped quietly into one of the seats on this almost empty bus we were on, took out his guitar and went right into "Raunchy".

'Some days later, I asked John: "Well, what do you think about George?"

'He gave it a second or two and then he replied. "Yeah man, he'd be great!" And that was that. George was in and we were on our way.'

After that, all they ever did was practise and practise. 'Where are we going lads?' John would suddenly cry out in the middle of one of these sessions. 'To the top!' they all yelled back.

'What is that then?' was John's next line.

'Why, to the toppermost of the poppermost!' was the final exchange, the baby Beatles' war cry.

Jacqui and I heard and saw it all. Our house became a refuge for them. Most of the other parents simply weren't prepared to put up with the pounding, constant, ear-splitting din.

'Julia was fantastic,' says Pete Shotton, John's great school-friend. 'We were always welcome at her house. She was a kindred spirit who told us all the nice things we wanted to hear. She never stopped encouraging us to try and go as far as we could.

'We all loved her because she did everything for laughs. She took nothing seriously, except having a good time. I remember her once walking up the road with us, wearing an old pair of spectacles with no lenses in. When we ran into someone she knew, she'd casually slip her finger through the frame and rub her eye, while we all fell about in the bushes cracking our sides. Julia was definitely one of a kind.'

John's visits to our house had never been regarded as 'special' in any way. They were simply part of everyday life. If Jacqui and I happened to be outside when he arrived, we simply shouted out 'Hi!' and carried on playing. He was there so often, his presence was a natural and familiar thing. He was simply our big brother who happened to have two homes. He often skipped school dinner and came to our house for lunch, sometimes with a friend or two. If *we* skipped it when we were older, then we either went home or to Mimi's. There would always be something waiting for us to eat. I remember Leila having her lunch with us almost daily for a long time. She had come to our house on the bus from school. No aunt was ever surprised if we just popped in. We were an interchangeable family, which is why John's home with Mimi was accepted by us.

But now John was beginning to spend more and more time at our house and his stays were becoming increasingly long. It's hard to judge how Mimi felt about him being with us so often. I only hope she was happy to see him finally rediscovering his mother. I vaguely suspect she may have been a little uneasy about the obvious differences in attitude between Julia and herself on the subject of bringing up children.

Mimi was a confirmed disciplinarian, who took her responsibilities as doyenne of the Stanley family seriously. She had very strict views about permissiveness and didn't approve of either John's increasing involvement with music or his newly adopted Teddy Boy fashion sense. Our mother, on the contrary, thought it was all terrific stuff. What John was attempting greatly appealed to her own rebel sense. She saw what fun it was to be able to thumb a nose at authority by the simple act of changing into drainpipes and a pair of winklepickers. If a bit of haircream could create such a delightful furore among grown ups, what kind of fuss might be created by a little impassioned rock and roll?

I shall never forget the hilarious bathroom jam sessions she shared with the budding Beatles. The bathroom in our little house in Blomfield Road was probably one of the smallest in Britain. To see John, Paul, George, Pete Shotton, Ivan Vaughan, my mother and probably a couple of hangers-on scrambling around inside, trying to find a place to sit, was like a comedy act.

They would be squeezed into the bath, perched on top of the loo seat, propped up against the handbasin, squatted on the floor, and standing with one leg up on the edge of the bath to support a guitar. Even getting the door closed was a feat. They sometimes went on for hours, letting rip into all those now classic tunes like 'Maggie May', 'Besame Mucho', 'Alleycat', and the theme music from The Third Man. My mother sometimes joined in on washboard, or playing percussion on an upturned saucepan or a pair of saucepan lid cymbals. The reason for their unusual venue was that the bathroom was the next best thing to

41

a proper studio. The wall tiles and the linoleum on the floor were perfect insulation, not unlike studio soundproofing. The acoustical effect was magnificent, even better than on Mimi's front porch.

'Those were the days!' Paul told me. 'We were really jammed in, couldn't move. Don't forget it wasn't only us in there, but all our instruments as well, and also a pig nose amplifier we carried around.

'It was the best room in the house, hands down. At home I used ours to practise in, too. When I actually had to go, I would lug my guitar in with me instead of a book. I remember my dad used to say, "Paul, what are you doing playing the guitar in the toilet?" And I'd reply, "Well, what's wrong with that then?" Many a fine tune has been written in that little room.'

The boys suddenly turned up once for a music session while Jacqui and I were having our bath, and we were promptly hauled out. That meant we could go and play until the session was over. Postponing bedtime was obligatory. It would have been impossible for us to get to sleep with the noise. Looking back, I realise we became a sort of refuge for John in his ever increasing struggle to live with Mimi amicably. Mimi, the aunt, was forced into the role of the heavy-handed mother which allowed Julia, the mother, to become the ever indulgent aunt. Besides, at heart, Julia was still almost a teenager herself who easily identified with John and his friends.

Mimi was very much the older sister, the unspoken and unchallenged leader, the one who advised and always had a shoulder to cry on. She was articulate, well-read and cultured, with a powerful personality. John was also developing a strong personality. Inevitably they fell out at times as he matured and began to assert his independence. I know he was happy living with Mimi. He was very fond of her and would never have hurt her intentionally. Mimi once told me that one day, when he was small, he was standing outside Mendips with her saying goodbye to our mother who was off back home.

'I do love you, Mummy,' he said as he kissed her. Then he paused for a moment, turned and looked at Mimi. 'But I do love you too, Mimi.'

* * *

On 15 July 1958 an absurd tragedy hit our family. I anticipated that something terrible was going to happen. That made it almost intolerably unbearable when I finally understood what my premonition had meant.

The evening started out ordinarily enough. My mother decided to visit Mimi, as she usually did at least once a week. It was all quite normal. Jacqui was in bed. I was playing in the garden with friends. John and my father, Bobby, were in the kitchen tidying up after tea.

The seven o'clock pips on the radio had just sounded. I was sitting on my bike in the front garden, getting my breath back after a race around the block. My mother came out of the door, called out cheerily, 'Just going to see Mimi, lovey,' and set off down the road to the bus stop. Nana, as we called Bobby's mother, our grandmother, followed her out of the gate a few seconds later and caught up with her. They were chatting away and my mother was laughing a lot at something Nana was telling her.

I can still see myself there. My bike was propped up against the gate and I was perched on the saddle, scuffing the toe of one sandal against the wall, watching the two of them walk away from me.

It was just another evening, nothing special. I had seen both my mother and my father walk up that same road dozens of times. When he was on his way to work, my father often turned to wave and blow us a kiss before rounding the corner.

Tonight, for no reason at all, I began to feel it wasn't quite the same. Suddenly, I knew something was terribly wrong. How does a child feel panic? My recollection is that my chest felt uncomfortably tight and I wanted to retch. Waves of fear swept through me, as if someone was standing over me, threatening me with a huge, hard fist. Without thinking, I threw down my bike and ran faster than I ever had to the top of the road, to try and catch my mother before she got on the bus. It was too late. When I turned the corner she was gone. I never saw her again.

She had arrived as expected at Mimi's house, and the two sat down for one of their long chats. Then, shortly after ten, my mother got up to go. Normally Mimi walked with her across

Menlove Avenue to the bus stop. Tonight Mimi said, 'I won't walk you tonight, Julia. I'll see you tomorrow.'

'Don't worry,' replied my mother, gave her a hug, and walked out of the door to Menlove Avenue, a dual carriageway directly outside the house. Nigel Whalley, who had the somewhat grand title of The Quarrymen's 'official manager', happened to be walking down the road as Julia came out of the garden gate. They stopped to say hello and then my mother stepped off the pavement and crossed to the central reservation. She had just started across the other side when a car hurled her up into the air. She was killed instantly. She was just 44.

Many years passed before John could bring himself to talk about that night. What he finally said was this: 'An hour or so after it happened a copper came to the door to let us know about the accident. It was awful, like some dreadful film where they ask you if you're the victim's son and all that. Well, I was, and I can tell you it was absolutely the worst night of my entire life.

'I lost my mother twice. Once as a child of five and then again at seventeen. It made me very, very bitter inside. I had just begun to re-establish a relationship with her when she was killed. We'd caught up on so much in just a few short years. We could communicate. We got on. Deep down inside, I thought, "Sod it! I've no real responsibilities to anyone now."

'Anyway, Bobby and I got a cab over to Sefton General Hospital where she was lying dead. I remember rabbiting on hysterically to the cabbie all the way there. Of course, there was no way I could ever bear to look at her. Bobby went in to see her for a few minutes, but it turned out to be too much for the poor sod and he finally broke down in my arms out in the lobby. I couldn't seem to cry, not then anyway. I suppose I was just frozen inside.'

When the accident happened, Jacqui and I had long been in bed fast asleep. I woke up to find Nana creeping into my big double bed. She always slept with me when she stayed the night. She cuddled up to me and I fell asleep, only to be woken again by the arrival of Jacqui in the bed.

A few minutes later we heard the most horrible sound coming from our parents' room next door. It was our father crying, dreadful racking sobs alternated with terrifying moans. It was very frightening. Nana snuggled us under the eiderdown and told us to go back to sleep. She went to comfort him. When we got up in the morning, Daddy was gone. 'Where's Mummy?' I asked Nana.

'Oh, she stayed with Mimi last night, that's all. Nothing to worry about, dear.'

Stayed with Mimi? She never did that. She was always here in the morning to give us breakfast. But there was no reason not to believe Nana. Grown-ups never told lies. It was bewildering.

At school, the atmosphere got worse. The headmaster, a kindly man, took us into his study and made a great fuss of us for most of the morning. The teachers came in, kissed us and cuddled us, and sat us on their knees. One took me to the girls' cloakroom and helped me wash my hands and face. At the age of eleven, I was quite capable of doing that for myself.

The overdose of kindness was sinister. I felt very, very frightened. 'What's happening? What's the matter?' I shouted out at the headmaster, terrified now.

'I'm afraid your mother has been in an accident. She's in hospital.'

The next shock was at home. Mater and Bert, our aunt and uncle from Edinburgh, were in my room packing our clothes into two large suitcases.

'You girls are coming up to Scotland for a holiday with us,' said Mater, all cheerful and normal. 'Isn't that lovely?' She lowered the tone of her voice. 'Your mother is very ill, you see, girls. So you won't be allowed to visit her just yet.'

She lifted her voice, back to cheerful Mater: 'Anyway, we're all going to have a lovely time together in Scotland.' Our father reappeared briefly and disappeared again. He looked pale and strange. 'Gone to visit Mummy in hospital,' explained Mater.

I find it very difficult to understand how they were able to go through such a terrible, unforgivable charade. It went on and on. After six weeks in Scotland we came back to Liverpool to stay with our aunt Harrie. The accident still hadn't been mentioned. Our enquiries about our mother were fobbed off, until we stopped asking. I knew she must be dead. As John once said, 'A conspiracy of silence speaks louder than words.'

Unknown to us, there had been a funeral. It had taken place in Allerton Cemetery, very near our home. The family can't have been aware how cruel they were excluding us from the communal family grief. We weren't babies. We were quite grown-up little girls. They must have realised that sooner or later we would have to be told. Perhaps they hoped that eventually we would completely forget about our mother and it would all go away. It was the old family maxim, Never Tell The Children. This time they got it more wrong than they ever had. Even now, as a woman of forty, I feel very resentful about the way the family behaved. Leila, my eldest cousin, was at Edinburgh University studying medicine. When it happened, she was on a summer vacation job working as a chalet maid at a Butlin's holiday camp. She received a telegram which said: JUDY CAR ACCIDENT. DIED FRIDAY. FUNERAL TUESDAY.

Says Leila, 'I set off for home immediately. All I could think was, "Poor John".

'I remember him and me going to the funeral in a complete daze. There seemed to be lots of people but I didn't recognise many. I couldn't stand it. I hated the funeral and everybody there. It was impossible to believe it was Julia in that box. It made me sick seeing all these strangers walking up to the grave and throwing flowers and handfuls of earth on to her coffin. I could only think of Julia at home, happy and laughing as she always was.

'Afterwards we all went back to my home, The Cottage, and John and I just sat there on the couch, him with his head on my lap. I never said a word. I can't even recall telling him I was sorry. There *was* nothing you could say. We were both numb with anguish.'

Eighteen months before, Paul McCartney had also lost his mother. She died suddenly from breast cancer, a month after it was diagnosed, because she hadn't complained about the pain until it was too late. I can hear my mother saying to John, 'You must bring Paul home for something to eat. Poor lad, losing his mother.' She felt so sorry for him. How ironic.

Paul says: 'When I look back on Julia's death, all I can see is the word TRAGEDY written in big black letters. The only way I could help John was to empathise, as I'd had the same thing happen to me. There wasn't anything I could say that would magically patch him up. That kind of hurt goes far too deep for words.

'About a year after a rather funny or, more accurately, a rather cruel incident happened. John was just beginning to get his act back together again. That is, he could bluff it out a bit better than before. He and I were out together and we met someone who happened to ask me how my mother was getting on.

' "Well, actually, she died three years ago," I said. He didn't know where to look. "Awfully sorry, son. Oh, my God."

'Then he turned to John and asked him the same question, only to be told precisely the same thing. As young lads, we both found his deep embarrassment rather amusing. Laughing about it was a wonderful way of masking our true feelings and gave us a bond.'

What made my mother's death worse was that the driver who hit her was an off-duty policeman suspected of drunken driving. At the inquest he was exonerated of any negligence and they recorded a verdict of Misadventure. All these details were still completely unknown to my sister and me, even two months later after we had gone to live with Harrie, Leila's mother, at The Cottage.

Harrie was two years younger than my mother and the youngest of the five sisters. Her husband, Norman, Leila's stepfather, worked as a garage manager. The Cottage was a small house attached to the dairy farm that had been previously owned by Mimi's husband's family. The main house and land had now been sold to a stocking factory and The Cottage had been absorbed into suburbia. Best thing of all for us living there was that it was very near Mimi's house and John.

Jacqui and I were trying to settle in, still as much in the dark as ever, when everything changed one morning after Norman called us both downstairs. He looked rather serious, and started by saying 'Sit down please, girls.' He gave several ahems and ums, as if he couldn't bear to get it off his chest, and then it came straight out. 'You won't be seeing your mother again, girls. She's in heaven.'

The brutal truth, presented like that with no frills, was

absolutely devastating. Jacqui and I immediately burst into uncontrollable hysterical screaming and sobbing. Harrie, upstairs making the beds, heard all the commotion and rushed into the sitting room. She realised at once what Norman had told us. 'How dare you!' she said. 'What right have you to tell them like that? What right have you to interfere with my family?'

'You can't make them go on like this forever,' said Norman. 'They had to know.'

Norman was right. We did have to know. How could they go on pretending we still had a mother when she was dead? But it should have come from our father. He was the one who should have told us at the very beginning, 'Mummy isn't coming back.'

But Daddy couldn't cope. He was totally shattered by her death. The very object of his existence had gone. He cried day and night for months afterwards. So the sisters took charge of everything, as they always did in a family crisis. I often wonder, if my father had been left to at least try and cope, could he have managed?

There was another problem, the attitude of the Fifties before the Sixties Revolution. Whatever he felt about his two little girls, men in those days simply didn't run both a job and a home. Had he wanted to defy convention, it would have been, in practical terms, very difficult. He worked late and at odd hours with his hotel job which wouldn't have fitted in with our regular school routine.

At least until I was sixteen, I remember my father becoming weepy at the mere mention of Julia's name. Her death devastated him beyond belief. Somehow he went through the motions of going to work but we often saw him depressed and withdrawn, not at all like the old Daddy we had known. He couldn't bear to stay on in our old house in Blomfield Road and within weeks he had moved to a house about half a mile from our new home in The Cottage, which meant we saw him at least a couple of times a week. Sometimes we went to stay with him. We had our own rooms, with the beds from our old home and all the books and toys we hadn't taken with us to Harrie's. I once crept into my father's room and looked into the wardrobe. Hanging inside were some of my mother's dresses, including her fluffy pink evening dress with the gold and silver stars and the polka dot navy blue and white dress she always wore around the house.

John didn't lose touch with my father. He and Paul often went over to visit him. One of the big attractions was my father's gramophone, the one John and our mother had used to play Elvis Presley records.

'We used to borrow it to listen to the latest Carl Perkins records we'd dug up in town,' says Paul.

'I remember catching hell from Bobby once for accidentally scratching a record that belonged to him.

'Bobby was a good bloke and always seemed to enjoy seeing John. But I do know John had this sort of stepfather thing about him. He liked him all right but he couldn't quite associate with him as his dad.'

At first the new life thrust on Jacqui and me at Harrie's was very difficult. We took a long time to get over the delayed shock of finding that our mother was not, as we had thought, still around. Things had seemed normal to us when my mother was alive – the focus of our family and a very doting one. Now we had moved to The Cottage, though, I knew we were different and could not come to terms with it because no one could talk about Mummy. She became a taboo subject, to be lived inside us. Children want desperately to be the same as all other children – a sheep-like quality. Now we too were living with an aunt, like John. I hated acknowledging this at school, because it meant acknowledging my mother's death. We were extremely well looked after, but it had all become different. One thing I dreaded in particular, because of this difference, was the signing of the School Report. Where it said Parent/Guardian at the bottom, my uncle would delete Parent and sign it. I was always enraged and humiliated. I had a parent, why didn't he sign it? But I could never bring myself to say anything at home. I'm sure it was never even considered as something that would give rise to such intense feeling in a schoolchild, but that's how it was. I was realising that we were not the same as most of the others I knew. The whole feeling is brought back regularly with my own children's reports, as I cross out Guardian, maybe too vehemently.

Having been on many visits to Woolton while our mother was

alive, we already knew Harrie well. Gradually, the wounds must have begun to heal. We became content. We now had a stable mother figure in Harrie, although of course she could never replace the one we had lost.

One of the great advantages of our new existence was a new brother, David, Harrie's child by Norman. His birthday fell between Jacqui's and mine and he was an ideal playmate to bridge the gap between our ages. David became one of my good friends and we have since spent much time together with our families.

Very slowly our father was also recovering. Never completely, but enough to start thinking more about us two girls.

There were the odd nights when we stayed with him. Then he suggested we move in for the whole of our next school holidays. Our bedrooms were all set up and Nana would always be around to look after us when he wasn't there. We did this for a couple of holidays, moving in with Harrie again when the term began to settle back into school.

The arrangement came to an end. Harrie thought it was unsettling. Daddy's house was very free and easy and discipline went by the board. He spoiled us rotten. She insisted for our own good that we had one home only. So we didn't go back the following holiday. The women in our family always did have the final say.

John was now seventeen, and no longer a schoolboy brother with time on his hands. He had earned the title of the School Bohemian, drop-out, whatever. He had been in various deep-end troubles with the staff and I remember him bragging to his friends at home about wearing two pairs of trousers for certain days and occasions – in other words, when he knew he was going to get caned: we all read *Just William* and *Billy Bunter*. He left school under rather a cloud. Mimi went to see the headmaster to discuss a future for John and then to the Liverpool Art School with John and a portfolio. He was accepted. I remember John saying that he wanted to be a commercial artist (my image was one of him standing on a tall ladder with buckets of paint, actually painting the advertisements up there!). I don't know whether that would have materialised, but I'm sure he could have made a successful life as a painter if the Beatles hadn't happened.

At Art College he began leading his own grown-up life and we saw much less of him. Now and again he dropped in at Harrie's house for a quick meal and some rough and tumble with Jacqui and me, who were still young enough and giggly enough to adore it. Sometimes his visits were simply an excuse for leisurely free phone calls. Harrie, with an eye on the telephone bill, naturally had an aversion to the use of the phone for what she felt were inessential purposes. John's calls must have come into this category because he always took great precautions to avoid being seen when he used it. He crawled out of the front window, telephone in his hand, and dragged the cord behind the rhododendrons where he settled down to long conversations. We never knew who all the calls were to. I suspect that many were 'over the water' to the Wirral, on the other side of the Mersey, because he started bringing round a girl who lived there called Cynthia Powell. They had met at art school, where they were in the same class. Cynthia was a lovely girl, shy and rather refined, and always very kind to Jacqui and me. John's friends were a bit put out though: Cynthia was far too respectable to fit into the image of a rock 'n' roller's moll.

John had his own ideas about his perfect woman. Soon after he and Cynthia started going out together, he made her dye her hair blonde so that she would look more like his fantasy sex symbol Brigitte Bardot. His Number Two pin-up was Juliet Greco but as Cynthia was also a brunette, he couldn't have made any sacrifices there.

Says Paul: 'Unfortunately for Cyn, she happened to come along at the time everyone was trying to turn their girlfriend into a bargain basement Bardot. We all happened to be at the age when a ravishing sex goddess taking off her clothes was *the* fantasy for us boys.

'We were all smitten. So the girls had to be blonde, look rather like Brigitte and preferably pout a lot.

'John and I used to have these secret talks intimating, although not actually saying it, that we could be quite happy for our girlfriends to be Liverpool's answer to Bardot.

'My girlfriend was called Dot and, of course, John had Cynthia. We got them both to go blonde and wear mini skirts. It's terrible really. But that's the way it was.'

Jacqui and I got to know Cynthia well. She and John were always round at The Cottage and seemed very much at home there. On Saturday afternoons they sat on the settee holding hands while we all watched television. Sometimes Harrie came in and sent us out of the room so that the two of them could be alone. After that, we couldn't wait for tea-time and the privilege of taking a tray in to them, with the added bonus of seeing what they were 'up to'.

They seemed to be very much in love, the picture of romance in my young eyes. But life wasn't always happy ever after, as I well knew from my limited experience.

ABOVE: George, Stuart
Sutcliffe and John
acting tough in
Hamburg, 1960

LEFT: All the family
went to watch The
Quarrymen
performing at the
Woolton Fête in 1956.
John met Paul
McCartney for the first
time that day

LEFT: The Quarrymen in action in Rosebery Street, Liverpool. Mummy took Jacqui and me to watch

RIGHT: The Silver Beatles at an audition with tour promoter Larry Parnes in 1962. Stuart Sutcliffe is far left, with Johnny Hutchinson on drums

LEFT: Mimi in 1963, still living at Mendips after John's initial success

John in Mimi's garden, holding Julian

Just-married John and Cynthia, 1962

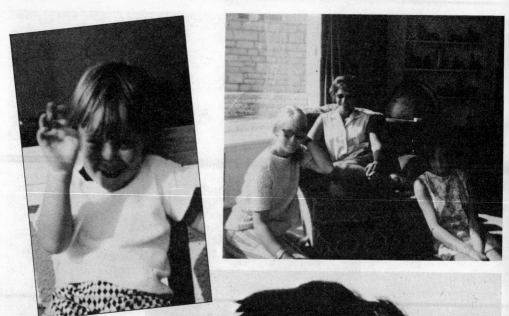

ABOVE LEFT: Julian in Bournemouth, aged 3

ABOVE RIGHT: Cynthia at Mimi's home in Bournemouth with Harriet and Jacqui, summer 1965

RIGHT: John sent Mimi this picture of himself from Hamburg. On the back he had written, 'Come hither-type look'!

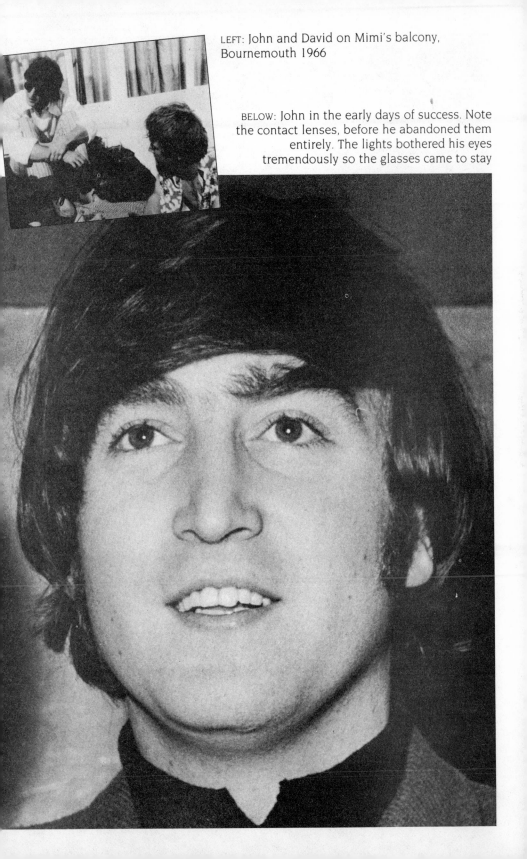

LEFT: John and David on Mimi's balcony, Bournemouth 1966

BELOW: John in the early days of success. Note the contact lenses, before he abandoned them entirely. The lights bothered his eyes tremendously so the glasses came to stay

BELOW LEFT: John and his coveted Rickenbacher guitar

BELOW: On stage during a Beatles world tour, 18 December 1965, not long before the group gave up life on the road

LEFT: Clowning with Paul at an English press conference, 1966

LEFT: A leap into the unknown during A *Hard Day's Night*, 1965

BELOW LEFT: Harrie and Mater sprucing up in front of a bemused Paul McCartney before an early Beatles concert

BELOW: 'Extra' performance during the filming of A *Hard Day's Night*, 1965

ABOVE: The Fab Four posing for the Beatle-hungry press on Loch Earn in Scotland, 1964

LEFT: John and George flying high during one of their world tours

BELOW: The Beatles meet the Prime Minister, Harold Wilson, in 1964

Chapter Three

LIVING ON A DREAM

'I started going to see the Beatles at the Cavern from the time I was about eleven. We lived right next door to John's mum for over ten years, but I was always afraid to say anything for fear he wouldn't remember me. Finally, I sent a girlfriend backstage to get his autograph and, of course, he was charming. On stage they were all just *brilliant*. The whole place used to literally vibrate when they were on. And they weren't stuck up either. Most groups left immediately after their set, but not them. They'd be there all night. Just sitting at the coffee bar, chatting, like anybody else.'

ANN STARKEY

'When we first came down to London we felt like real provincials. But it really was a great period, we were like the kings of the jungle. It was probably the *best* period, actually, fame wise. We didn't get mobbed so much. It reminded me of an exclusive men's smoking club, you know, only with the Stones, Eric Burdon, and us as members. It was just a very, very good scene.'

JOHN LENNON

'We loved it like mad when we were first starting out because all we ever wanted was to go around Liverpool and be cute and popular, play our guitars and not have to work. But once it really became over the top we were forced to take a closer look. Was this really what we wanted? Shooting round the world locked in the back of armoured cars and leaping about like performing fleas in baseball arenas. After a while, the Beatles simply became an excuse for people to go around behaving like animals.'

GEORGE HARRISON

John was a long way off being a millionaire, but the little money he did earn from the Quarrymen gigs gave him an element of independence. In 1959 he decided to move out of Mimi's and share a flat with Stuart Sutcliffe, a talented art student in the same year as him at college.

Compared to Mimi's extremely comfortable house, Stuart's flat at Number 3 Gambier Terrace was a real student pad. The view was splendid enough – it overlooked Liverpool's Anglican Cathedral – but the inside was a bohemian jungle of half-finished canvases, unmade beds, paints and brushes in every available corner, and familiar bachelor piles of unwashed dishes. Mimi naturally hated John leaving home and did her best to persuade him back to a civilised existence at Mendips. But John liked the new-found freedom of having a place of his own where he could play the guitar as much as he liked. He still went back to see Mimi at least once a week, to have his laundry done and enjoy a good home-cooked meal, and she finally accepted he wasn't going to change his mind. He enjoyed the unconventional student life he shared with Stuart and, besides, it meant that he and Cynthia now had a place to be alone together.

John and Stuart had a close friendship, based on mutual admiration. Stuart was a dedicated artist with undeniable talent and John greatly admired his superior ability. John on the other hand was a forceful, charismatic personality exploring artistic avenues as yet unknown to the quieter-natured Stuart.

In many ways they were complementary to each other. Stuart opened up the world of painting to John, while John introduced Stuart to music by teaching him to play the bass guitar. The Quarrymen renamed themselves. With Paul and George at the Liverpool Institute, and John no longer at Quarry Bank, the old name had no relevance, and they became the Silver Beatles. John thought it up. Beatles was chosen to reflect John's affection for Buddy Holly and the Crickets, but spelt with an 'A' to indicate Beat music. Silver was an added grand touch which was dropped a couple of months later.

They were short of a bass guitarist and, at John's suggestion, his new pupil joined them. But Stuart's mastery of the guitar left much to be desired and there was considerable friction as a consequence, especially between Stuart and Paul McCartney. Paul explained it to me like this: 'I admit I had problems with Stu. I regret it, of course, as he is now dead, but sometimes you can't help these things if you run up against controversy. It was mainly because he couldn't really play very well which made it very embarrassing when we were on stage or having photos taken. We had to ask him to turn away from the audience or the camera, so it couldn't be seen that his fingers weren't in the same key as the rest of us, or how few chords he could play. I was probably over fussy but I felt it wasn't a good thing for an aspiring group to have such an obviously weak link.

'Stuart was really a lovely guy and a great painter, but he was the one I used to have all the ding-dongs with.

'One time we even had a fight on stage. I assumed I'd win because he wasn't all that well built. Some extraordinary power must have taken him over because he was not an easy match, let me tell you. We were locked for what seemed ages. "I'll kill you, you bastard!" I screamed at him. "I'll bloody get you, McCartney!" he screamed back. I think they had to pour water on us in the end.'

Despite the growing pains, the Beatles started doing more and more engagements at socials and working men's clubs and sessions in clubs like the Cavern and the Casbah which were springing up all over Liverpool. Pete Best had joined the group as their new drummer and the Casbah was the basement club in his mother Mona's house in West Derby, a suburb of Liverpool. Lots of people went there, as well as to the Cavern, although I was too young myself. It is still open now and can be visited by fans of the era.

The Beatles rapidly developed a devoted local following. In

August 1960, club owner Allan Williams was asked by Bruno Koschmeider, the owner of a German nightclub, to supply several Liverpool groups over a period of two or three years. Williams chose the Beatles and they were invited to Hamburg for an extended engagement on the notorious Reeperbahn, the main street in the city's stripclub quarter.

Hamburg was hardly a taste of the good things to come. Their audiences were drunken and unruly and they had to play very loudly to get any attention at all.

The five of them – John, Paul, George, Stuart and Pete Best – were accommodated not in a hotel as they expected, but in a single cramped room behind the screen of the Bambi cinema. If they had a long night and slept in late, they found themselves woken up by the sounds of the first showing.

It was rough and money was tight, but Hamburg proved excellent experience musically. At home in Liverpool they were used to playing for an hour at the longest, limiting their repertoire to only their best tunes. In Hamburg their new bosses made good use of them. Sometimes gigs went on for as long as eight hours which meant they had to extend themselves and find new ways of playing. It was a hard day's night but they couldn't help but get good with so much practice.

'Our peak for playing live was in Hamburg,' recalls George. 'At the time we weren't famous and people came to see us simply because of our music and the atmosphere we created. We got very tight as a band in those four clubs we played in Hamburg. First was the Indra, and when that closed we moved over to a larger club called the Kaiserkeller. Later we went to the Top Ten, probably the best place on the Reeperbahn, which had a natural echo and was a gas. The Star Club was very rough but we really enjoyed ourselves there as well. Playing such long hours we developed a big repertoire of our own songs, but still played mainly old rock 'n' roll tunes.

'In England all the bands were getting into wearing matching ties and handkerchiefs, and doing little dance routines like the Shadows did. We definitely weren't into that bit and so we just kept on doing whatever we felt like. Ultimately I guess it worked out okay.'

Those five months in Hamburg changed both their music and the boys themselves. None of them had seen this seedy, raw side of life before.

Having little in common with the beer swilling Germans who were their usual customers, they fell in with Hamburg's arty crowd. One of them was beautiful Astrid Kirchherr, a photographer's assistant, and Stuart fell madly in love with her.

Astrid and her two friends, commercial artist Klaus Voormann and photographer Jürgen Vollmer, saw the Beatles as something more than simply cabaret background to the sleazy clubs they worked in. They recognised their potential for much larger, popular audiences. They began to photograph the Beatles both as a group and individually in different locations around the Reeperbahn.

The boys made a demonstration disc in Hamburg at the Akustik Studio which led nowhere. It was very amateurish, rather like the one they had made as The Quarrymen in a friend's basement studio in Liverpool.

On their second trip to Hamburg the following April, they were invited to do the backing for a record with Tony Sheridan, the British singer at the Top Ten Club. It was being produced by Bert Kaempfert, the German orchestra leader, for Polydor. They recorded six numbers backing Tony, and a further two on their own, 'My Bonnie' and 'Cry For a Shadow'. That session meant a lot to them. No longer could anyone say they were just a scruffy rock band posing as professionals. They had made a real record, not some demo disc cut for the dustbin. It was the deluge of requests for 'My Bonnie' that persuaded Brian Epstein, a wealthy Liverpool record retailer, to go and hear them play at the Cavern. Subsequently, of course, he became their manager.

Stuart wasn't at the recording session. He had decided to leave the Beatles, stay on in Hamburg permanently, enrol at the Art College, and marry Astrid. The Beatles went back to Liverpool and left Stuart to his new life. John and he wrote long letters to each other. Suddenly Stuart, only twenty years old, died in Hamburg from a brain haemorrhage. His death hit John badly. He had never had a friend as close as Stuart. His death following so

LIVING ON A DREAM

close to our mother's must have been very hard for John to bear.

After that, we all felt back in Liverpool that he seemed to be drawing closer than ever to Cynthia. In Germany the other Beatles had already noticed his commitment to their relationship. Cynthia was in charge of the savings fund for their future and every week without fail he had gone off to the Post Office to send her money. In his little spare time, beyond the long hours the Beatles already worked, John often freelanced on his own outside the group, playing guitar accompaniment to the local strippers. Anything extra, after beer money and living expenses were cared for, went to Cynthia. Outwardly John appeared to be the same aggressive young man many people had always known. But Pete Best remembers John's soft centre, especially when it came to his feelings about Cynthia.

Says Pete: 'There were moments in Hamburg when John and I would really talk. Sometimes the two of us went out for a couple of quiet beers and chat about our plans for the future.

'He used to tell me how he and Cyn planned to settle down and raise a family as soon as the Beatles began to pay off, and how much he missed being without her. There were definitely two sides to John. One was the outrageous guy on stage who continually lost his temper, took the mickey out of everyone, and generally acted the goat. The other side which the public didn't often see was really very gentle and tender, most of all when he was talking about Cyn.'

Jacqui and I began to feel the effects of the Beatles' growing success. They were now famous enough locally for our school-friends to be extremely envious that we were related to John. We were constantly asked to get photographs, autographs and records, and bizarre mementos like a pair of John's old socks or a lock of George's hair. A quick look at John's bedroom at Mendips was another frequent request. The lucky ones got an exercise book signed. We couldn't see what all the fuss was about, although it was fun to be considered important contacts of such sought-after boys. As we saw it, John was just a big brother doing the sort of thing big brothers did, but who would one day have a proper job. The grown-ups in the family were quite unconvinced that stardom was in store. They decided the Beatles were just a fad. It couldn't possibly mean anything more than it obviously was, youngsters larking about in those new-fangled clubs playing guitars for pocket money. As long as they didn't get into any trouble it was harmless enough, but it was in no way considered to be any sort of career.

They refused to take any of it seriously, especially Mimi. She was thoroughly fed up by now with girls – John called them Beatlettes – coming round to Mendips chasing after him. One of the Beatlettes was a girl in my class called Linda. She made a real effort. She managed to manipulate her way into Mendips by soft-talking Mimi with a great deal of skill, and she was actually invited to breakfast. She felt that was a great coup, as indeed it was, to overcome Mimi's natural resistance to these first hints of Beatlemania. 'I went and had breakfast with John,' Linda told me at school that morning, with a great deal of pride in her voice.

The teachers began to ask us, 'Is that your brother?' and we slowly realised that the Beatles were making quite a name for themselves. Finally the family had to reconsider that perhaps they had it wrong, even Mimi, and that John and the Beatles were really on to something after all.

I was fifteen years old, and big enough to go into Liverpool with four or five friends from school to see John at the Cavern in Matthew Street. The din was unbelievable. Most people don't realise how very small the Cavern was. It was in the cellar of an old warehouse near the docks and the walls were dripping with damp which ran down in streaming black rivulets. There was hardly any light and you had to grope your way to the so-called bar where the strongest drink they served was Coke.

Everyone was dressed in black, Cathy McGowan-style. Cathy McGowan was the 'hip' presenter of *Ready Steady Go*, screened a lifetime ago on Friday evenings. It was one of the forerunners of the pop music programmes on television today. She became a cult figure for a time, sporting long, black hair with a fringe well down on the eyes. Many imitated this style. My hair was subjected to the ironing board on several occasions, as it was far too wiry to be right! We all wore black on black – black eye make-up with a pan-stick foundation – a close imitation of the

60

Munsters I'm sure! Black polo-necks and dyed black jeans were the order of the day (they didn't make black jeans then). The more like a corpse you looked the better. Getting out of the house like that was difficult. We had to apply the final dramatic touches around the corner out of sight. You were supposed to be eighteen, and a couple of times I was told I couldn't go in unless I went back home for my birth certificate. But most of the time, if you applied your make-up expertly enough, the doorman would be totally confused by your appearance and let you in.

'At the beginning the Beatles played at the Cavern lunch-time sessions only,' says Bob Wooler, one of the Cavern's first comperes. 'Ray McFall, the owner, was very reluctant to give them a chance and I really had to talk him into it. Probably the only reason he finally agreed was that they were one of the only local bands available to work during the day, as they were all virtually unemployed.'

Paddy Delany, the Cavern's huge doorman, was well built for the job of keeping out undesirables. He remembers the Beatles as having 'a certain animal magnetism and a raw vibrancy to their music.'

Paddy saw and heard everything that went on, and had followed the Beatles' progress from the beginning. Ringo Starr's replacement of Pete Best on drums came as no big surprise to him. 'It was inevitable,' says Paddy. 'Pete wouldn't conform to the style Brian Epstein wanted for them. He also didn't believe in a lot of things the boys may have been into at the time. All in all, he was very badly done by, which is a shame because he really was a very good-looking fellow. The girls at the Cavern used to say he reminded them of Jeff Chandler.'

It seems a shame that Pete Best missed out just on the eve of fame, since he was a friend of John's and I know they always got on well. On the other hand, where would the Beatles have been without Ringo Starr?

Mike McGear, formerly Michael McCartney, Paul's brother, looks at the whole affair philosophically. 'It could have been any one of them that fate chose to go,' he says. 'None of them was that strong. But when they all got together, that's when the magic happened.

'The other three were very quick but, remember, Pete was exceedingly good-looking. The girls screamed for him and that was a great asset. They wouldn't have sacked him for that. No, it was all down to his drumming capability in the end. There were quite a few good drummers around Liverpool and I used to go home and tell Paul about Ringo who I often saw playing with Rory Storm and the Hurricanes. He certainly hadn't Pete's looks, but he was an amazing drummer. He went at the drums like crazy. He didn't just hit them, he invented new sounds.'

In the summer of 1962, just as Ringo joined them, the Beatles started their meteoric rise to fame. In August John had some unexpected news when he called in to see Cynthia at her flat in Garmoyle Street near Penny Lane. She told him she had just discovered she was pregnant.

'Don't worry, Cyn,' said John. 'We'll get married.'

When Mimi heard the news, she was furious. It was probably the biggest row she and John had ever had. 'You stupid children,' she told him. 'Getting yourselves into this situation. No one in the family will ever have anything to do with you again. Well, it's on your own heads now. You got yourself into it, now it's up to you to try and put things right.' It was an emotional reaction, and understandable. Poor Mimi must have wondered if she would ever be free from coping with family plights. Gradually she calmed down and reluctantly came to terms with the situation. She wasn't happy about it being a shotgun wedding but, as always, her overwhelming sense of responsibility overcame her disapproval. She even gave John the money to buy the wedding ring, a simple gold band which cost ten pounds in Whitechapel, one of the main shopping streets in the city centre.

The night before the wedding, that same month, John started to have second thoughts. 'Oh, Christ, I don't really want to get married, Mimi,' he moaned, pacing up and down Mendips' well-ordered sitting room. 'I'm too damn young.'

'Maybe so,' said Mimi coldly. 'But what's done is done.'

The next morning, 23 August, John was a typically nervous bridegroom, the same as any other twenty-one-year-old taking the plunge. Mimi chose not to attend the wedding and there was only a handful of other guests, among them Paul and George,

Brian Epstein, and Cynthia's brother Tony and his wife. As usual, the children of the family weren't invited. After all, Cynthia had been a naughty girl!

'It was more like a funeral than a wedding,' says Cynthia in her autobiography, A *Twist of Lennon*. 'John, George and Paul were huddled together in one corner of the drably decorated waiting room. All of them wore black suits, white shirts and black ties. Their faces were pale and strained, their hands fidgeted nervously, alternately adjusting their ties and loosening their collars, or running their hands through their well-combed hair – almost in unison! John's family stuck to their decision to boycott the occasion – a sad statement of their lack of understanding.

'We were ready to begin. John and I looked straight ahead out of the window, and in the backyard of the adjoining building was a workman firmly grasping in his hands a pneumatic drill. As if on cue, the moment the ceremony commenced he began drilling. None of us heard a word of the service; we couldn't even hear ourselves think. Trying to keep straight faces and our minds on the enormity of the step we were taking was an impossibility. All we wanted to do was get out and have it over with as soon as possible. It was all totally unreal.'

In October 1962, Brian Epstein signed the Beatles to a five-year contract, and began to develop the Beatle look. Producer George Martin at Parlophone, one of EMI's smaller companies, had already given the Beatles a recording test. John had only been a husband for a fortnight when George invited them down to London to EMI's Abbey Road studios in St John's Wood to make their first British record in September 1962. It was 'Love Me Do', with 'PS I Love You' on the B side. About a week later, I remember climbing up the stairs to my cousin David's room in The Cottage, where Jacqui and I lived with Harrie, clutching John's demonstration disc of 'Love Me Do'. It was so exciting hearing them on a real record. In my eyes they were now every bit as important as Elvis Presley – even if, to my ears, they didn't sound like a professional group.

'Love Me Do' was officially released in October 1962. The entire family, Mimi included, were thrilled beyond words. 'I've always said that boy could do anything he set his mind to,' Mimi kept

saying with enormous pride, quite forgetting her original pre-
dictions for John's future as a musician.

It was great having a famous brother, but one thing bothered
me. I was very concerned that my friends would find out about
our complicated family, and my having to explain it all. For an
adult, it would be a simple matter to explain that John was the
offspring of our mother's first marriage, and that he lived in a
different house. For a self-conscious fifteen-year-old, terrified of
being thought 'different', it was an extremely sensitive subject.

The show-down I dreaded never happened. But everyone at
school continued to talk non-stop about the Beatles. Even part
of the official school notice-board was devoted to their
movements, as now they were going on tours throughout the
North. But it was still their regular appearances at the Cavern
which excited the Liverpool fans most.

Another great occasion was hearing the Beatles on Radio
Luxembourg for the first time on 12 October. The reception was
so faint and crackly we had to crouch round the radio, cupping
our ears to pick out the music from the terrible static coming
through the speaker. It didn't spoil the excitement. There was my
big brother on the radio, being listened to by thousands of
people. I couldn't help thinking how much our mother would
have liked being there with us. The following January, when
'Please Please Me' was released, I remember us all booing Jimmy
Saville when he introduced it on his programme. 'Well, here it is,'
said Jimmy, 'the big new record from Liverpool's Beatles. I sure
hope it pleases somebody out there, 'cause it sure isn't me.' I
wonder how many times Jimmy has regretted that particular
remark.

On 8 April 1963, seven months after the wedding, John Charles
Julian Lennon was born at 7.45 am at Sefton General Hospital,
Liverpool. The Julian was after our mother. It was a long labour
that left Cynthia exhausted, without John there to support her.
He was away on tour in the south of England, but he had been
telephoning Mendips every night to see how Cynthia was. He was
thrilled when Mimi told him he had a son.

'When can I see him, Mimi?' he shouted excitedly down the
phone.

'Don't worry,' Mimi told him. 'They'll both be here when you are. Just get home as soon as you can.'

After the birth, Cynthia asked to be moved to a private room. The Fab Four already had such a legion of fans that a newborn Beatle son in a public ward would have caused an uproar. It wasn't much better in the private room. The only one available was framed by two large picture windows which did little to protect Cynthia's privacy from the gathering fans outside. Brian Epstein decided that a married Beatle, like any married pop star, wasn't good for a business which relied so heavily on female supporters. He insisted that little Julian's arrival be kept as low key as possible. That was pretty difficult in the circumstance because everyone seemed to know about it. His son was a day old when John met him for the first time. He fell over himself with excitement, hugging and kissing Cynthia and the baby at the same time, unable to contain his joy. 'Who's going to be a famous little rocker like his dad?' he cooed. 'He's bloody marvellous, Cyn.'

Julian was barely three weeks old when the Beatles took their first holiday after months of non-stop work. Paul, George and Ringo flew off to Tenerife in the Canary Islands to join some German friends. John told Cynthia he was going to Spain with Brian Epstein for a ten-day break before the Beatles resumed their demanding tour schedule.

Cynthia wasn't exactly pleased to be left behind, but Julian was too small to travel, and she realised John needed a break after working so hard. In the month of April alone – which was typical of their work schedule that year – the Beatles did a total of thirty concert, television and radio engagements.

It was that same Spanish holiday which caused a terrible fight at Paul's twenty-first birthday party two months later, in June. It was fairly drunken and tempers were running high. Bob Wooler, the Beatles' old disc-jockey friend, insinuated that John was having an affair with Brian Epstein, who was known to be homosexual. John went for him. Bob ended up in hospital with three broken ribs and an out of court settlement from John of £200 damages. From what I know of John, he wasn't the least bit homosexual. Quite the opposite.

It was a tough life on the road. With Brian pushing them all the way to the top, they never stopped working. At first Cynthia didn't join John on tour. He wanted her to stay at home so that Julian could lead as normal a family life as possible. Besides, Brian wasn't anxious to have her along with them, his views on married Beatles being just as adamant. At both their insistence she agreed to stay in the background. After Julian's birth, she had moved out of the little flat she and John had first shared together, and into Mendips. It was a lonely life for her there.

The Beatles' name had become a household word in Liverpool. Fans were always likely to pounce on her if ever she went out with Julian in the pram. She always denied any connection with John, laying low for the sake of John as Brian had suggested. It was a difficult role to play, being a wife who wasn't supposed to exist.

Julian wasn't an easy baby. He was always crying and refused to train to any sort of early routine. 'I was left quite alone desperately trying to cope with a baby that seemed to cry all the time,' says Cynthia. 'I ended up a nervous wreck trying to keep him quiet, knowing Mimi wouldn't be having a minute's peace. I used to wrap him up and push his pram to the very end of the garden and just let him scream after I had done everything possible for him. I hoped and prayed he would tire himself out so that I could catch up on my sleep. In the end, I was so exhausted I was actually seeing double. John was really on to a good thing, being absent from the joys of fatherhood in those early stages!

'It was all very well, because when he did come home he would leave the room whenever I changed a nappy. He said that if he had stayed he would have been sick, and if he had had to put up with crying night after night I am sure he would have left home.'

John began to realise this wasn't much of a life for Cynthia. As Julian got bigger, Cynthia started to go on tour with him occasionally. I can personally attest to the power of his lungs.

Cynthia often left Julian with Harrie when she went away. Harrie was the youngest of the Stanley sisters, the baby-crazy aunt who revelled in her role as official family baby-sitter. We used to come home from school and suddenly find Julian's pram in the hall and nappies drying around the fire. That meant Cynthia had gone off to join John.

Beatlemania had engulfed Great Britain, and now proceeded to engulf the world. We began to see less and less of John, although we always knew where he was and what he was up to. When John moved Cynthia and Julian to a new home in the South in July 1964, they went out of our day-to-day lives on a permanent basis.

Like everyone else, we used to read about him in the newspapers almost daily. He kept in regular touch with Mimi on the phone, sometimes chatting to her for hours at a time, just as he and I did later on, towards the end of his life.

We naturally missed him being around and the non-stop lunacy that went with having a brother like John. The next best thing was having his name and photograph splashed all over the papers. In a way, it gave both Jacqui and me a great sense of optimism about our own lives. We had seen how hard John had tried to make it, and how he had finally got his reward. It was a salutary lesson in determination. If you wanted something badly enough, then it would be yours in the end if you were prepared to work for it. The Quarrymen and then the Beatles had hung on year after year, despite the disappointments, confident they would make it – and they did. It was fantastic to realise that our brother had, in his own words, reached the toppermost of the poppermost.

We felt an enormous sense of pride that it was he who wrote and played popular music better than almost anyone else had ever before.

Now that Beatlemania had taken over the world, fans from all over the world came to hang around Mimi's house, knocking on her door at all hours of the day and night. They camped on the grass verge outside the garden gate, set up tents, played guitars and sang Beatle songs. Every time she went out she had to force her way through tents and sleeping bags. Mendips had become a shrine to Beatlemania and Mimi was being driven quite mad.

One day John suggested that it might be best if Mimi put Mendips up for sale and found another, more private place away from all the madness. Privacy, as the Beatles themselves had begun to find out, was a highly desirable ingredient of life. Mimi didn't want to move. She loved her home. She had lived there for thirty years and now she was being pestered out of it.

After John and Cynthia moved away from Liverpool, Mimi often went to London to see him. She was there one morning in August 1965, when John suddenly announced that his chauffeur was picking them up to take them house-hunting. Mimi protested, saying she didn't want him squandering his money as she was really quite all right in Mendips, despite the fans.

'But if you *were* going to move, Mimi, where would you like to go?' John asked.

Wracking her brains for something to say, she announced for no reason at all: 'Bournemouth'. They immediately set off with the chauffeur, and in Poole, near Bournemouth, John spotted a luxury two-tier bungalow, with steps leading down from the garden to the sea. Mimi and John went inside and met the owners. The sale was arranged. Mendips was put on the market. The people who bought Mendips didn't realise what they were in for. The fans continued to lay siege. Coachloads arrived on guided Beatles tours and megaphones blared out the history of John's childhood days. Now, peace appears to have come at last. A notice has been erected outside Mendips which reads: 'Official Notice. Private. No Admission. By order of Merseyside County Council.'

Mimi settled into her new home. The house was secluded and she couldn't be overlooked. Only sometimes during the summer season did she hear a megaphone from one of the pleasure steamers crossing Poole Bay. 'That white house is where John Lennon's aunt Mimi lives.' If Mimi happened to be in the garden, everyone on board started waving like mad. It didn't particularly bother her as otherwise she was quite uninterrupted and the audience was ship-bound.

It was a wrench leaving Liverpool and the rest of the family. John finally talked her into it by persuading her what a great holiday home it would be for the whole family, with plenty of room for us to stay if she wanted company.

'John was always generous to a fault,' Mimi often said when repeating the story of her move to Bournemouth. 'Even as a child, if he happened to have only one small bar of chocolate but two friends with him, then right into thirds it would go without so much as a blink.'

I know how true that was. John's generosity became legendary. He was too warm-hearted to say No. He was always thinking up ways he could help out once he had the money to do it with. Some time later, in 1968, he told Harrie to go and find a bigger house because The Cottage was too cramped with five of us living there.

After looking at various houses, Harrie found her ideal one on a private estate in the smart Woolton area where Ringo Starr had bought his parents a house. John bought ours without hesitation. He told Harrie she could do what she liked with it in the way of furnishing and equipment. Just send all the bills to him, he said. It had every mod con imaginable, unlike the charming but rickety old Cottage. There was an ultra modern kitchen, wood-block floors throughout; a brand new, detached house. It was John's way of letting us know that, even though he wasn't around, he was still concerned about us.

The Liverpool première of A Hard Day's Night in July 1964 really brought home to me the phenomenon of Beatlemania and John's incredible success. Sisters, cousins, aunts, uncles – we all went, and none of us had ever experienced anything like it.

John first kitted us up. Jacqui and I chose pigskin, made to our own design by one of John's former Art College friends who had set up a leatherware business. I decided on a full length black pigskin coat lined with red silk. It was the most glamorous item of clothing I have ever owned in my life. The material alone cost £80, a fortune then, and more like ten times that by today's prices. Jacqui later cut it up to make a fringed jacket.

A shiny black limousine was sent to each of our houses to chauffeur us through Liverpool to the civic reception at the Town Hall. The streets were packed with cheering, waving people, like the crowds that line the route at a royal wedding. What excitement we felt being at the receiving end of all the attention!

At the Town Hall the Lord Mayor was waiting in his red regalia and gold chain of office to present its heroes to Liverpool. Inside, we could only hear a continuous muffled roar. Then the Town Hall servants in their civic livery flung open the windows to the balcony overlooking Castle Street. I had seen pictures of the Queen standing on the balcony of Buckingham Palace after the Coronation and I realised then how she must have felt. The cheering and the screaming was so loud we couldn't hear ourselves speak. Over 200,000 people were there, according to the *Liverpool Echo* next morning. They were everywhere, up trees, clinging to lampposts, standing on walls. The Beatles were at the front of the balcony, waving like mad as the fans continued to scream their lungs out. I remember peeking past John's shoulders at the sea of faces and thinking they looked like a sea of sugar puffs, just like at school when you looked down on assembly from the stage. I kept hoping no one from school was there. A vain chance that was! It was an unbelievable experience standing there on the balcony, waving back like royalty, knowing John was the focal point of it all. Here was a man whose name was now known throughout the world by kings and queens and almost every famous person you could think of, and by everyone who read a newspaper, or listened to radio, or watched television: it hardly seemed possible that it was my brother. The Beatles had hit the headlines so many times, we had long since stopped cutting out stories about John from the papers.

The next item on the agenda of that amazing day was a magnificent feast laid on by the City Fathers for its four famous sons. It was laid out in the Town Hall's main reception room under glittering chandeliers and a ceiling encrusted with gold leaf. Champagne, smoked salmon, caviar, chicken breasts, hors d'oeuvres of endless variety and quantity. We couldn't stop ogling. Harrie was keeping a close eye on us as we made a bee line for the goodies. 'Don't be eating all that food yourselves,' she warned. 'A bit of decorum please. You're here to celebrate your brother's success, not to fill yourselves up.'

Afterwards we left for the film première at the Odeon with the other guests. All the top stars of the day had come, like Tommy Steele, Lionel Blair and Alma Cogan. As if we hadn't eaten enough already, we were all given a large box of chocolates to eat while we watched the film. Before it started, the Beatles came on to the stage to a tumultuous roar from the audience. We still couldn't believe it was all happening. 'Where's me family?' John

70

shouted out. 'I can't see any of you.' We waved and shouted back as loud as we could, and all the audience started laughing.

What we didn't realise at the time was that life was like this *all* the time for the Beatles. Wherever they went, whatever they did, even if it was simply walking down the street, fans were always there hysterically shouting and screaming. Unless they were behind doors, they never had any peace at any time of the day or night. They were always under siege.

It was especially bad on tour when they had to lock themselves into their rooms as hordes of fans stormed the hotel outside. Finally John decided it would be safer for Cynthia and Julian to live outside London, in a remote part of the affluent suburbs, away from the constant hysteria. 'Kenwood', a mock-Tudor mansion, was their first big house. Bought in July 1964, it was on the exclusive St George's Hill Estate in Weybridge, in the Surrey stockbroker belt.

Kenwood was already lavishly fitted out when John bought it. Even so, John insisted on renovating it completely. He spent nearly twice as much again as the original cost of the house changing rooms around, knocking down walls and redecorating.

'The first nine months in our new home were spent occupying the staff flat at the top of the house', remembers Cynthia. 'An army of workmen arrived and proceeded to tear the place apart. The beautiful designs that were presented to us seemed a long way from reality as we wandered through rubble-filled rooms with ripped up floorboards and what seemed like hundreds of workmen's tin mugs and billy cans. In fact *we* were the mugs. I can't remember inspecting the house when the men were working, they always seemed to be sitting there gossiping and drinking endless cups of tea. I felt like a foreigner in my own home. I kept having to remind myself that we were the ones paying for it all.' When they began to get the house straighter, John arranged for Jacqui and me to go down for a few days. We loved the idea of being with John again at long last. It was an added bonus when he sent us air tickets: we'd never been on a plane before.

The grand finale to that first flight was our reception at Heathrow Airport. A uniformed chauffeur was waiting with John's brand-new Phantom V Rolls Royce to drive us home to Kenwood. Such VIP treatment for two schoolgirls from Liverpool was pretty cool stuff, as was Kenwood itself. Gliding up the long drive towards it, we were impressed by what we saw. It was a mansion-sized, mock-Tudor house on a slight hill, surrounded by a landscaped garden with trees and shrubs and manicured lawns, like a scene from *Homes and Gardens* magazine. John being rich was something Jacqui and I never thought about. This made us realise exactly what being a Beatle meant.

The main hall was dominated by an elegant oak staircase and opening off it were the reception rooms, all beautifully furnished. John's den off the sitting room was entirely decorated in red and lined with books. John was an avid reader, a habit encouraged in his childhood by Mimi, and Cynthia said he often sat in there for hours with his nose in a book. One important room was missing: Cynthia's ultra modern dream kitchen. Somehow the builders hadn't got around to it yet. A dug up floor on the other side of a great hole in the wall was the only indication of where it was to be one day. In the meantime, meals had to be cooked upstairs in the flat where the housekeeper and her husband, the chauffeur, lived and brought downstairs to the dining room.

The builders were still building and dust was flying every-where, but nevertheless John was a stickler for doing things properly. He insisted we eat formally in the oak panelled dining room, underneath a sparkling chandelier on a beautiful oval mahogany table. Never mind if it was just a boiled egg for breakfast, we had to do it the right way. Bringing the meals two floors down from the housekeeper's flat and keeping them hot was a terrible palaver. Most families would have opted for a casual meal on laps under the circumstances. Not John. Julian was now big enough to sit up at the table in his high chair and John, despite many of his unconventional attitudes, maintained old-fashioned principles. Julian had to be taught to eat properly. I once got into trouble over lunch because I pulled a face at Julian and jokingly stuck my tongue out. 'Stop that,' John growled at me. 'He will copy you and I don't want him doing that.'

John and Cynthia's room was one of six bedrooms upstairs. It was carpeted in white and had an ensuite bathroom with a sunken bath. We had never seen such luxury.

Julian had a full-size rocking horse in his nursery which he was too small to sit on without falling off. It was more than big enough to bear my weight, sitting on it with Julian in front.

Everything in the house was lavish and large. In the sitting room, beautiful leaded-glass panes dominated the wall which overlooked the garden. You could see the stables which John was having rebuilt and a large swimming pool, sadly not in use because John had designed an elaborate psychedelic eye which was being set in tiles on the bottom.

John was obviously very proud of his new house. He told us one day: 'Mimi's often implied I just struck lucky with the Beatles, sort of like winning the pools or something. But I think she might just be beginning to see how hard we've worked to deserve what we have, especially after joining us this summer on our Far East Tour.' The Beatles had performed in Hong Kong, Australia and New Zealand in June 1964. That short holiday with John at Kenwood meant a lot to Jacqui and me. It was great being a family together again. Fantastic though the house was, we'd have been just as happy if it had been the gardener's cottage. The important thing was being with John. We had a family life at Harrie's of course. But it wasn't the same as having our own proper family, like John, with us. It was almost as if Mummy might come waltzing in through Cynthia's kitchen hole in the wall with a trayful of scones straight from the oven, humming a nonsense tune.

On the sitting room floor were some bulging canvas sacks which really intrigued us. Cynthia explained that they contained John's fan mail and invited us to have a look. We spent several hours totally absorbed reading through some of the thousands of letters. They were a fascinating insight into how passionately the fans felt about the Beatles. Nearly all of them were from girls.

My darling John,
I must make this letter short as there are tears in my eyes. I could never love or marry anyone else. No other arms will ever

hold me. No other lips will ever kiss me because to me you are a Greek god. You are the Ninth Wonder of the World.
Loving you is all I do,
Karen R.
Seattle, Washington

Dear John,
You are too skinny. You should eat pizza or lasagna to fatten up. Then there would be more of you for more of us.
Worried,
Anne Marie D.
Freeport, Louisiana

Beatle John,
What about girls who have braces on their teeth, wear glasses, are very plump, and have lots of freckles? Do they still stand a chance?
Hopefully,
Margaret K.
Pittsburgh

We decided to reply to a few, explaining we were friends of John's. I like to think the girls who got an answer were pleasantly surprised and didn't mind us being John's stand-ins. They surely must have realised the impossibility of any of the Beatles replying to the hundreds of letters which arrived every day from all over the world.

I think Cynthia enjoyed our company. She often spent long weeks on her own when John was away touring or spending endless hours recording at the EMI Studios. It must have been lonely for her in that house, surrounded by all the luxury and having no one to share it with.

Happily John was there quite often when we went to stay. His main preoccupation at that moment was learning to drive. It was something he had never done. When he had the time to learn to drive, he hadn't the money to buy a car. Now it was the other way around. He had three cars (a black Ferrari and an all-white Mini with electric windows, as well as the Rolls) but couldn't take them out on his own as he hadn't passed his test. That didn't stop him from wanting to take us for a drive. We were horrified. We were convinced he would have an accident. What would the police do if they caught him out?

'No problem about that,' he told us. 'We're going for a spin on the local golf course. No danger at all of getting nicked. I'm a Beatle!'

Off we sped over the golf course, careering up and down the fairways and through the sand bunkers with a disrespect for the sanctity of the course which would have horrified the members of the golf club. Fortunately it was too early in the morning for any of them to be out playing, and we never were able to test John's theory of Beatle infallibility.

John began some more recording sessions in London and we ended up spending a lot of time with Cynthia. She was a kind person. She wasn't at all pushy or ambitious, and never had been as far as John was concerned. She seemed happy with him as he was. She hadn't let the money go to her head and she was as natural as ever. I always felt that had things worked out differently between her and John, she and I might have become friends. Sadly, after she and John split up, I saw her only twice more; once at Harrie's funeral in 1972, and once at John's request.

They were happy days we all had together, walking along the banks of the Thames, Julian in the pushchair, feeding the ducks and having picnics. A couple of times the chauffeur drove us three girls into London for a shopping spree at Harrods and Harvey Nichols in Knightsbridge. Money was no object. It didn't seem to matter how much we spent. We could have anything we wanted. That put Jacqui and me in a slightly embarrassing position as we were frightened to admire anything too much. If we did, Cynthia simply whipped her cheque book out of her bag and insisted we have it. Each time she did write a cheque, it was fun to see all the whispering and nudging between the assistants as they recognised the name. We bought blouses, cashmere sweaters, leather trousers, and a new outfit each for the Beatles concert John was taking us to later in the week. We were loaded with bags when we left. At the store exit we had some right royal treatment from the Harrods doorman in his green and gold uniform who was waiting to open the door of the Rolls and help us in. It was the first time I saw ladies handing their dogs to a doorman at Harrods. Amazing!

One Sunday, John took us to see George and Pattie Harrison. They lived in a long, low bungalow called 'Kinfauns' which had a heated swimming pool and was on a private estate in Esher. Cynthia did the driving – even John had to admit she was considerably safer on the roads than he was.

Cynthia and Pattie had become friends. Living so close to each other and having Beatle husbands in common, it was a natural friendship. Besides, neither felt embarrassed at the other's wealth, which often set them apart from other less fortunate and sometimes envious friends. We had seen Pattie often, although never met her. As Pattie Boyd the model, she had been a familiar pretty face on TV, advertising potato crisps. Jacqui and I couldn't get over being in Pattie's house, when previously we had seen her at Woolworth's in Liverpool doing a promotion as the Smith's Crisps girl.

The house was very contemporary with pinewood furniture and huge coloured cushions on the floor, Indian-style, instead of chairs. We all sat on the floor, Jacqui and I chatting and listening to music as the others talked together. We couldn't help thinking about next week when John was taking us to our first Beatle concert.

Our introduction to Beatlemania in the raw wasn't just different, it was mind blowing. It was in 1964, and the Beatles were playing at the Finsbury Park Astoria in London. In the car, I sensed John was edgy. But then I didn't know what was in store both for him, and for Jacqui and me.

The theatre was surrounded by a seething, screaming crowd. The noise was horrendous and very frightening. The Rolls slowed down and a sea of faces and flaying arms came at us in waves, pushing forward time and time again as a wall of policemen with linked arms battled to hold them back. The chauffeur was well used to it all. With great skill he manoeuvred the Rolls and aligned the passenger door with the stage door entrance, so that we could spill out without being engulfed by the crowd.

The dressing room was tranquillity itself. The boys were sitting around drinking Coke, apparently unconcerned about the frenzy outside. Mick Jagger was there, and I was very impressed with that. Then someone put their head around the door and shouted, 'Ten minutes. They're going crazy. They're wild out there.'

The first four rows of the theatre had been cordoned off and left empty, as a safety precaution to keep the fans well away from the stage. They were too busy screaming their heads off to notice Jacqui and me being lowered from the side of the stage to take our seats there. The minute the Beatles came on stage, all hell broke loose. Despite sitting right in the front, we couldn't hear any singing at all. The hysterical screaming drowned every sound but the very loudest bars of music. Suddenly people started pushing towards the stage, scrambling over the seats, jostling around us, shoving and screaming at the same time. I had seen the Stones in Liverpool, but nothing had been like this.

Then John shouted out between numbers, 'Get the girls. Now!', and we were being pulled out of our seats and back on to the stage by two of the Beatles' security men. We watched the rest from the wings, the safest place to be at a live Beatle concert. It was a madhouse and it made me wonder at the tremendous pressures they were under the whole time.

On another visit down South, John took us to our first recording session at the EMI studios in Abbey Road where they were working on the 'Day Tripper'/'We Can Work It Out' single for release the next month. It was November 1965 and Beatlemania still hadn't burned itself out. That meant our approach to the lovely Georgian mansion that housed the studios was as hazardous as ever. A crowd of Beatle fans spotted us while we were stuck in the traffic and raced along beside the Rolls, right on through the studio gate. 'Can I have your autograph? Please!' begged one little girl who couldn't have been more than twelve. 'Why me?' I asked her. 'Because you're with *him.*'

While John and the boys got to work in the studio, Jacqui, Cynthia and I were shown into the control room. We were joined by producer George Martin and his chief engineer Norman Smith who had been out on the floor making last-minute adjustments to the amps and microphones.

Everyone thought making music came easily to the Fab Four,

but it didn't always. It often took time for the creative juices to start flowing, as we began to see now.

This was their second session on the track. Already a good deal of work had gone into it, and still more was needed before the Beatles finally came up with anything that could even remotely be called music. After what seemed like an eternity of tuning, all that came through the speakers in the control room were dissonant guitar chords, bits of vocal harmony and a few half-hearted run throughs.

After three hours, we'd had enough and decided on a walk outside. We wandered off down the road, skirting around the fans who knew we were with *him*, and pondered on the strange experience. How could anything as brilliant as the Beatles' music be born out of such a disjointed and tuneless hotchpotch?

When we got back to the studio, a new sound greeted us. The musical liquorice allsorts had been magically transformed into 'Day Tripper'. It had taken a total of eight hours non-stop grind to produce three minutes of music. John earned his living the hard way, whatever anyone else thought.

That same year, 1965, Alf Lennon made a comeback. He decided the time was right to reappear out of the blue and lay claim to fame as John's long-lost father.

Paul McCartney was always close to John on family matters, both their mothers having died within such a short time of each other. He told me what had happened.

'I first got to know about it from an article in the *Sunday People*, something about "Beatles dad washes dishes at the Greyhound Hotel in Hampton Court".

'I was with John when he read it. He just kind of went, "Oooohhhh . . ." Fortunately we both had a sense of humour and managed to laugh it off. Eventually, though, John did agree to see him.'

What distressed John was that Alf had never once tried to make contact since 1945, when John was only five years old, and that the Beatles' success had finally prompted him to do so. Alf was obviously not a pop fan because he said he had had no idea about John's amazing career until a workmate pointed out a newspaper photograph. 'If that's not your son, Alf Lennon, then I don't know what!' he told him.

Immediately after that, stories about Alf started to appear in the newspapers, although Alf steadfastly denied he had deliberately sought publicity. 'I couldn't help it,' he explained.

'I never saw him until I made a lot of money and he came back,' said John later. 'I opened the paper and there he was, working in a small hotel very near where I was living in Weybridge. He had been writing to me for some time before that, trying to make contact. I didn't want to see him though. I was too upset about what he'd done to me and my mother, and the fact that he hadn't bothered to turn up until I was rich and famous.

'Originally I wasn't going to see him at all, but he sort of blackmailed me in the press by saying he was a poor old man washing dishes while I was living in luxury. I fell for it and saw him and I suppose we had some kind of relationship.'

After their first meeting, John was quite encouraged. He told his old friend Pete Shotton, 'He's good news, Pete. A real funny guy, a loony just like me.'

The relationship quickly turned sour when Cynthia invited Alf for an overnight visit to Kenwood. One night turned into an extended stay of three days and with it some highly emotional scenes between John and Alf.

Alf succeeded in making John really furious when he teamed up with small-time record producer Tony Cartwright. Together they cooked up an outrageous scheme to promote Alf as a pop singer. Unlikely as it was, they even managed to land him a record deal with Pye for his one and only single, 'That's My Life (My Love and My Home)', under the Piccadilly label. Like son, like father. 'That's My Life' was released exactly four weeks after the Beatles' *Rubber Soul* LP which carried John's autobiographical track, 'In My Life'. The almost identical title of Alf's record and the timing of its release was too much of a coincidence. But Alf, as ever, was ready to talk his way out of any situation. He sent promotional copies of his record to all the top DJs and showbiz editors with a glowing press release. He started to call himself Freddie, now the more fashionable derivation of Alfred.

'Fifty-three-year-old Freddie Lennon, father of John, has made his first record,' read Alf's press blurb. 'Mr Lennon has been an entertainer in an amateur capacity for most of his life. He comes from a musical family, for his father was one of the original Kentucky Minstrels, and taught him to sing when he was young. When he left the sea twelve years ago, Freddie took a job as a waiter, and later worked in holiday camps at various northern resorts. He came to live in London seven years ago. Over the years, Freddie was always interested in songwriting, but he never took it seriously. Six months ago he met Tony Cartwright, who is now his manager. Together they wrote "That's My Life", a story of Freddie's life. The song was accepted by a music publisher and eventually recorded.'

'That's My Life' delighted the disc jockeys. Musically it wasn't much, but for curiosity value alone it was excellent air time. John was very embarrassed that his father was making such a fool of himself and, even worse, laying himself open to accusations of cashing in on his son's name. John's anger was mostly directed towards Alf's manager, Tony. By encouraging Alf to do the record, John felt that Tony was taking advantage of Alf's innocence in the world of show business.

To cap it all, Piccadilly Records issued publicity photographs of Alf attempting to play the guitar with his all but toothless mouth wide open in song. John was very sensitive and deeply family minded and he hated the public ridicule his father had been exposed to. I felt very hurt for John over what happened with Alf. I remember thinking, 'I'm glad he's not *my* father.'

The next time Alf showed up at Kenwood, John turned him away in disgust. Charlie Lennon, Alf's younger brother, explains how everything came to a head. 'As soon as Alf's record started moving up the charts, Brian Epstein stepped in and somehow got control of his contract from the record company. Before you knew it, the record had all but disappeared from view. Tony Cartwright and Alf went off to see John about it at his home, but he just slammed the door in their faces. Later that night Alf rang me in Birmingham and told me all about it. He said he was sure John wouldn't have turned him away if he had gone on his own, without Tony. Alf was obviously very hurt. He told me, "It was a mistake to have got involved with any of this in the first place."

'Frankly, I was a little miffed at John for treating his dad that way, so I wrote him a stinking letter for acting such a child. His response was a totally unexpected phone call inviting me down to Kenwood for a visit. "Why not take some time off and come and see your childish nephew, Uncle Charlie," he said.

'It was difficult getting out of work that particular weekend, but I managed and went down there from Birmingham. John was out on film work when I arrived and I spent the afternoon chatting with Cynthia.

'John came home that evening happy as a lark, going on and on about how he really thought deep down his dad was great, despite what anyone said. At that point I didn't dare mention the letter, in case he decided to punch me in the face or worse.

'Despite everything, I know Alf was genuinely proud of John. He often told me, "My son's a typical Lennon alright. The talent's in the family. Just look at our dad. Our mother always used to say that if only they could have afforded a piano, then somebody in the family would definitely have become a pianist."'

Three years later, in January 1968, Alf contacted John once again, this time with the good news that he planned to marry a nineteen-year-old Beatle fan called Pauline Jones. Even Charlie, Alf's own brother, was shocked to hear of the forthcoming nuptials. 'Nineteen years old? You could have knocked me down with a feather,' says Charlie. 'I said to him, "Isn't one broken marriage enough for you? Don't you ever learn? She's young enough to be your granddaughter." But Alf didn't listen, he never did.'

Alf's bride-to-be was a student at Exeter University but she had given up her academic career on her impending marriage. Alf told John that Pauline was a bright girl. Perhaps, Alf suggested hopefully, John could employ her as his personal assistant as soon as she was Mrs Lennon. John couldn't say no to anyone, not even Alf, the cause of so much misery.

The new Mrs Lennon started work, but it didn't last. After five months she was dismissed. But John continued to care about his father's welfare and bought him a £15,000 house near Kew

81

Gardens in West London. He also paid for Alf's new place to be
furnished and gave him a £30 a week allowance. Alf never was
satisfied. Not long afterwards, he and Pauline decided to move to
Brighton, where John continued to pay part of their living
expenses.

Alf and Pauline's first son, David, was born at about the same
time as John and Yoko's marriage in 1969. David was barely a year
old when Alf decided it might be rather nice for him to meet his
big half-brother.

Alf decided on a surprise visit to Tittenhurst Park, John and
Yoko's new home in a rambling 70-acre estate in Ascot,
Berkshire. It was an unwise decision. Alf's unexpected visit came
at a particularly troublesome time in John and Yoko's turbulent
life together. Besides, Yoko wasn't that anxious to meet her new
toddler brother-in-law. Once again there were cross words and
Alf was shown the door.

Strangely, underneath his anger, John continued to show
concern for the father he had never really known. When Alf was
taken to hospital a few years later, dying of cancer, John was on
the phone to him every night.

Alf was too ill to speak, but John prattled on talking about the
family and his mother Julia. When Alf died on 1 April 1976, John
offered to pay the funeral expenses. Pauline, to her credit,
wouldn't let him. She said she felt that, as Alf's widow, that at
least was her responsibility. John, sad and weary by now of saying
goodbye, didn't attend the funeral.

By 1966, the Beatles had all but given up touring in favour of the
privacy and sanctuary of the recording studio. Live concerts with
their hysterical audiences were both demanding physically and
limiting artistically. Brian Epstein and his management team
weren't happy about their decision. But the Beatles had had
enough. After three years on the road, coping with screaming
fans around the world, always being the constant focus of
attention, they had reached breaking point.

Even worse, some people began to regard their musical ability
as having a god-like power. Desperate parents with ill and
crippled children would come to the stage door, begging the

Beatles to touch them so that they could be healed. The power of Beatlemania began to terrify them. They wanted to run away and become normal people again.

Anything any one of them said, however casually, became a statement of fact. They had become the world's most important four people, whose deliverances were almost as consequential as those of the President of the United States or the head of the Soviet Union. A prime example was John's controversial remark about the Beatles being 'more popular than Jesus'. Fanned by the press, the controversy reached its peak during their American tour which, as it turned out, was their last ever.

'We had a rough tour,' Paul McCartney told me. 'After John's bigger than Jesus quote, we suddenly had all the Ku Klux Klansmen burning our records on crosses and people marching around protesting about us. As a tour, it wasn't particularly worse than any of the others, but we'd had enough. Our concerts sold out, and the individual shows were great. But some people were continually trying to knock us. I remember John and George getting really pissed off at the whole thing. So we simply decided to give up all the hassle and work in the studio.'

Taken in its right context, John's remark was not blasphemous, despite what people thought. He was making a statement of fact, not out of any arrogance but as a realistic observation of the way so many young people felt about the Beatles. It *was* sadly true that the fans expressed far greater enthusiasm for going to a Beatles concert than they did for going to church. I know John was a little frightened by the reaction to what he had said. He hadn't realised what enormous influence the Beatles wielded outside their own sphere. The responsibility was too much. They were not politicians or manipulators, and if the pressure was on for them to be something more than entertainers they couldn't accept it. They decided to get out of the public eye, and on 29 August 1966 gave their last live concert performance at Candlestick Park in San Francisco.

Chapter Four

SEPARATE LIVES

'I have a great fear of this so-called "normal" thing. You know, the ones that passed their exams, the ones who went to their jobs, the ones that didn't become rock and rollers, the ones that settled for it. Settled for "the deal". That's what I'm trying to avoid. But I'm sick of avoiding it through my own self-destruction. I've decided now that I want to live. I'd actually decided it long before but I didn't really know what it meant until now. It's taken me many years to get this far though and I'm not about to give it up. I want to have a real go at it this time.'

JOHN LENNON

As I have never met her, I have no tangible relationship with Yoko Ono. Quite simply, we have never been together in the right place at the right time, or any place at any time. We did talk on the telephone a few times, but only when John and I were on the line to each other and Yoko chipped in on an extension.

In any case, we would probably have had little in common, apart from John. She never seemed particularly anxious to let us share John with her, as Cynthia had been. When John went to live with her in America, he lost touch with the entire family.

My brother first met Yoko in London where she was living at the time with her American husband Anthony Cox and their daughter Kyoko. The date of that decisive encounter was 9 November 1966. John had gone to a private preview of her one-woman art show, 'Unfinished Paintings and Objects', at the Indica Gallery in Mason's Yard off Piccadilly, and they were introduced by gallery owner John Dunbar, husband of Marianne Faithfull.

Their meeting came at a time when John was seeking direction to his life. The physical demands and mental stress of ten years of live concerts had taken their toll and the ill-effects of drug-taking were beginning to tell on him. He was looking for a new sense of purpose and Yoko was the impetus. His relationship with her was either to alter or emphasise many of his pre-conceived ideas about music, art, politics, women, career and family.

Yoko was a little-known avant-garde artist whose zany charisma totally enchanted John. He found he could communicate with her on an intellectual level; such as he had never been able to do with any other woman before. Cynthia was entirely different. For all her virtues as a wife and mother, she was conservative and unworldly. She admits herself, 'At times I did give a very boring, practical impression of being just an ordinary housewife instead of a swinging, extrovert pop star's consort.'

John was knocked out by Yoko. 'I've never known love like this before,' he proclaimed some months later. 'It hit me so hard that I had to halt my marriage to Cynthia immediately. Don't think this was a reckless decision because I thought very deeply about it and the implications involved. When we are free, and we hope that will be within a year, we shall marry.

'Of course, there is no real need to marry, but there's nothing lost either. Some may say my decision is selfish. Well, I don't think it is.

'There's another thing to consider, too. Isn't it better to avoid bringing up children in the atmosphere of a strained relationship? My marriage to Cyn was not unhappy, but it was a marital state where nothing happened which we continued to sustain. You sustain it until you meet someone who suddenly sets you alight.

'With Yoko I really knew love for the first time. Initially our attraction was a mental one and then it happened physically too. Both are essential in the union, but I never dreamed I would marry again. Now the thought of it seems so easy.'

John's decision to abandon his lovely English wife for a Japanese artist wasn't a popular one. Cynthia, who had been in love with John from almost the first moment she set eyes on him at Art College was incredibly understanding about his desertion. I admire her attitude tremendously.

'I didn't blame John or Yoko,' she says. 'I understood their love. I knew there was no way I could ever fight the unity of mind and body that they had with each other. Their all-consuming love had no time for pain or unhappiness. Yoko did not take John away from me because he had never really been mine.'

When the family heard about the impending break-up, they were naturally very upset. But no one doubted for a moment that John would do exactly as he pleased. He was a very positive man.

He had decided on a course of action and would pursue it. The main concern the family had was for Julian and Cynthia and what it would mean for them. We had always liked Cynthia and it had been fun watching my little nephew grow up.

Cynthia sued for divorce on 22 August 1968, on the grounds of John's adultery with Yoko, which he didn't contest.

In November, two weeks after Cynthia was granted a decree nisi in the London Divorce Court, Yoko miscarried the baby she and John were expecting the following February.

I felt very sad for Cynthia, knowing how much she still cared about John. The inevitable publicity that went with the first Beatle divorce made it even worse for her. To be rejected by your husband was bad enough; to be so publicly rejected in scream-ing headlines was dire humiliation. She disappeared from sight and we later discovered she had gone to Italy to nurse her wounds in the arms of hotel heir Roberto Bassanini. She married him, two years after the divorce, in July 1970 in the Kensington Register Office, West London. But she and Julian weren't happy with the jet set lifestyle favoured by the wealthy Italian. They were divorced after a very short time. Cynthia, at heart still very much a Liverpool girl, returned with Julian to Merseyside and bought a bungalow on the smart side of the Wirral, the peninsula between the Mersey and Dee estuaries.

My life on the other hand had definitely taken a turn for the better. In 1965, at the age of eighteen, I had just met Allen Baird. Allen was still at school in Northern Ireland taking his A levels and planned to go on to Queen's University, Belfast, to read psychology. I was two years older and about to embark on my degree course at Chester College to study French and linguistics. We had both decided to take a summer holiday job, and that is how we met at Butlin's Holiday Camp in Pwllheli, North Wales.

Allen was working as a cook and I as a chalet maid, just as my cousin Leila had been doing the summer my mother was killed. Allen and I hit it off instantly. He was a charming Irishman, full of fun and highly intelligent. Within days of meeting we were already planning to see each other again the next holidays. After an emotional parting I left for Chester to start my first term and Allen went back to school in Belfast. When he came back to England the following Christmas, I introduced him to my father. They got on well but my father was worried about me committing myself at such a tender age. 'Please don't get too serious,' he told me. 'You are both much too young.'

Over the last year I had begun to rediscover my father as the same supportive parent he always had been before my mother's death. We were building up a good relationship and for the first time in ten years he was at last able to talk about Mummy without breaking down. Although he seemed happy and cheerful, I sensed that deep down he was very lonely and was still greatly missing my mother all these years later. I don't think he ever really got over her.

He did decide to settle down again, though. Her name was Rona and I admit I wasn't very good or understanding about it at the time. Now that Jacqui and I had him back, we didn't want to share him. Besides, it was difficult to think of him being close to anyone but Mummy or us. It took a good friend of mine to make me see how unreasonable I was being.

'Face up to it, Julia,' she said. 'Your father's got a right to be happy. You are being very selfish.'

She was right of course. But I still felt threatened by his new relationship with Rona.

My father was a very charming man. He often drove down from Liverpool in his old Jaguar to see me at college, where he was a great hit with my fellow girl students. They gathered around and made a huge fuss of him and said they found it difficult to believe he really was my father. We spent a lot of time together and became very good friends. When I was short of cash, which I often was as a student, he fixed me up with part-time weekend jobs at the New Bear's Paw pub in Liverpool which he ran. He was as generous as always and gave me all the tips we made, just as he had John, from the large kitty bottle kept on the bar. After work, we often had a drink and a chat in a quiet corner of the lounge. It was there he introduced me to port and lemonade, a really delicious drink. 'But you mustn't drink too much,' he used to say. He was drinking a lot himself after hours.

Early one February morning in 1966, one of my father's old drinking chums, a man called Harry, turned up at college asking for me. One of my fellow students met him by the college entrance and brought him over to my accommodation block, where she asked him to wait while she ran in to tell me. 'Julia, come quick. There's a man outside called Harry who wants to see you and he's very, very drunk.'

I think I already knew then. I dashed outside and found Harry crouched down on the ground with his head in his hands, his body shaking with sobs. Harry lifted his head, the most dreadful look of anguish on his face. 'I've come to tell you,' he stammered through his sobs, 'I've come to tell you . . . your father is dead.' I was devastated. I couldn't believe what he was saying. I kept staring at him, trying to comprehend, and then the terrible reality slowly sank in as he told me Daddy had been killed six hours earlier in a car crash. I was stunned. It had happened twice. Two car accidents. And now both my parents were dead. My aunt, Nanny, telephoned the college at that precise moment to repeat the news. I threw on my clothes and my friend offered to take me back on the train to Liverpool. When I got there, Jacqui already knew.

There was nothing we could do but try somehow to comfort each other. I didn't go to the funeral. I couldn't have done. The pain was too much. Mummy and now him. Losing them both in the same unbearable way was incomprehensible. The anguish of his death only served to rekindle the anguish of hers. For a long time afterwards I was in shock, mourning both my father and, yet again, my mother.

It had happened as my father and Rona were on their way back after a night out with some friends in Ruthin, North Wales, which was about an hour's drive from Liverpool. They left it rather late and set off back home at about 1 am. It was drizzling and it was quite misty, but they got safely back into Liverpool. As they turned into Penny Lane, about a mile from their home, the car suddenly swung out of control and crashed into a lamppost. Rona suffered minor cuts and bruises, but my father died from his injuries in hospital soon after he was admitted.

Attempting to pick up the pieces of my life yet again, I went back to college with only my own family to reassure me there was still some sanity left in the world.

Allen, my future husband, now knew that John Lennon was my brother, although it wasn't something I had told him immediately. That may seem strange, but I have always remained silent about my connection with John. While I am very proud he *was* my brother, I always felt that my personal relationship with him wasn't important to anyone else.

John's fame was John's fame and only affected me as far as I let it. At school, it was a known fact, therefore I faced more questions about it; generally genuine interest in how the Beatles were faring. It was all very exciting at that stage, teachers and pupils alike wanting to know. Some whole double A level lessons were taken up discussing their progress at the time.

One or two people in the latter part of his life came to regard their connection with him as a status symbol. That was never the case for me. I had no wish to try and live in John's shadow. I had my own life to live and my own *modus vivendi*. Paul McCartney's brother, Michael, had also wanted to be a person in his own right. When he started working with the group called Scaffold, he changed his name to Mike McGear in case anyone thought he was cashing in on Paul's name.

When I began at Chester College, the *Liverpool Echo* decided to print a story about 'Lennon's Sister' in Chester College. I crossed my fingers that no one had read this red hot piece of news. I wanted to keep a low profile and enjoy my time at university unmolested by Beatlemaniacs or questions.

It wasn't likely that they had. Students came to the college from all over Britain and it was a long shot they had read any of the local Liverpool papers. I hadn't counted on Helen, a girl in the same accommodation block as me, who not only came from Liverpool but was also the girlfriend of the *Echo* reporter who had written the story. Helen introduced herself at the beginning of term and told me she knew who I was. '*Please* don't tell a single soul,' I begged her. 'I don't want any hassle.' She didn't and I spent the following three years studying in peace.

At the time I met Allen, my determination not to go through life merely as 'John Lennon's sister' was already rooted. I discovered early on that luckily he wasn't a particular fan of the Beatles. His tastes ran more to jazz musicians like Charlie Byrd and Stan Getz. I knew I would have to tell him about John at some time. It was ridiculous not being able to talk to your boyfriend about your own brother, just because he was famous.

One evening after work at Butlin's, we had decided to go to the pictures. There wasn't much choice because there was only one cinema in the village. And what else were they showing but A Hard Day's Night. I could hardly spoil our date by announcing I had already seen it, as an honoured guest at the Liverpool première.

After it was over, we started discussing pop music in general and Allen asked if I knew Them, the Belfast group. 'The drummer is a good friend of mine,' he said. 'Has been for years.'

'Really!' I replied. 'That's great, but I am very much afraid I can go one better. John Lennon of the Beatles is my brother.'

He was completely taken aback. You should have seen the look of amazement on his face. Of course, Allen was good about my secret after that. He never let on. He took the same view as me that whatever reputation a close relative had, for good or bad, it was apart from your own life. There was one time when *not* talking about my relationship with John was extremely difficult. It happened at a New Year's Eve party in Liverpool when I was introduced to a girl I had never seen before. We began chatting and she went on to confide that, although I must promise not to say a word to anyone, she was really John Lennon's long-lost cousin. Beatlemania gave some people extraordinary delusions.

Allen and I remained close throughout my college days. Every summer we went to France for working holidays, because I am a Francophile. When I passed my exams, Allen was still at Queen's with two more years of study in front of him. I needed a job and filled in forms for a post as translator at the United Nations in Geneva. We talked it over and realised we just couldn't be apart for all that time. I had told Harrie of our plans to marry and she began the laborious guest list and talked of 'next year'. We went back to Belfast, moved into a flat, and arranged to get married immediately on a three-week marriage licence. It all happened so quickly, I only had time to ring up Nanny the night before the wedding to let her know, and ask her to spread the news to the rest of the family.

We worked hard setting ourselves up in our new home. While Allen studied and worked in part-time jobs, I took a post as French teacher at a local secondary school. My sister Jacqui, now a trained hairdresser, had been working at Scissors in the King's Road, Chelsea. But like many people who make the move to London she got exhausted by living in the Big Smoke. She was soon back in Woolton again, working in a Liverpool salon. She and I were always very close to each other despite distances, which I suppose isn't so surprising as we have shared so much unhappiness and so many ups and downs together. Living in separate places did nothing to keep us apart. We were always on the phone to each other and she often came over on the ferry to see us in Belfast.

In 1970 Nicolas, the first of my three children, was born. That same spring John and Yoko came up from London for a sentimental journey back to Liverpool. It should have been the obvious moment for Yoko and me to meet, but Nicholas was only a few weeks old and I couldn't get away for a long time. After that, there never was another chance to meet her.

The family told me all about their visit later. They arrived in great style in John's white Rolls Royce. He had at last passed his driving test, but not without some perseverance on his part. They toured around his boyhood haunts in Woolton, Penny Lane and the centre of Liverpool, and John showed Yoko all the Beatles' old stamping grounds. The Rolls caused quite a stir. Everyone quickly realised who was inside when it rolled up outside our old house in Blomfield Road in Springwood, where we had lived with our mother and where the Beatles had their bathroom jam sessions.

The new occupant, Georgie Wood, who took over the tenancy of the house from my father, was delighted and proud to see them. Most Beatle fans already know Georgie's name as the imaginary crooner sung about by Paul in Let It Be, the Beatles' last album.

Their final stop was Harrie's and she was thrilled to have them to stay. All the neighbours looked through their windows at John's magnificent machine and wondered what on earth a Rolls was doing parked outside the Birchs'. 'But no one really caught on,' says Uncle Norman. 'Only one young lad next door figured out what was happening and dropped off a demonstration tape, which his own rock band had made, at the front door.'

John rang me up from Harrie's. He sounded really excited to be back in Liverpool again. He asked me about Allen, whom he had never met, and wanted to hear all about our new baby. He was very worried we were living in Belfast and wanted to know about the troubles. I told him we were perfectly alright as we lived in Finaghy, which was a Belfast suburb, and there hadn't been any problems there then. I was amused to hear that Yoko had been bending Uncle Norman's ear on the philosophy of zen.

I'd had no contact with John since his involvement with Yoko and it was great to talk to him again. He was so easy to chat to because he was such a warm, intelligently witty person.

John was a well-built man, but when Harrie saw him she became very concerned. 'He was incredibly thin,' she told me later. 'He's a mere skeleton of the boy we all knew.' Harrie was a great cook and her pièce de resistance was her Sunday dinners. She decided to give John and Yoko the full works. She went out of her way to produce a traditional celebration dinner in their honour with roast leg of lamb, gravy, garden-grown mint sauce, roast potatoes and vegetables, and home-made apple pie with cream for pudding. Just as delicious smells from the oven were beginning to waft through the house, Yoko announced that she and John weren't eating 'that sort of thing' anymore. They now ate only a macrobiotic diet, she said.

Harrie watched most disapprovingly as Yoko started to prepare a macrobiotic meal with diced fresh vegetables which she then steamed in Tamari sauce and served up to John with a lilliputian portion of organic brown rice. 'Chopping up carrots when all John needed inside him was a good meal,' commented Harrie.

Roast lamb had always been John's favourite and he must have been sorely tempted. But, as Harrie observed, he was so devoted to Yoko he would have made any sacrifice for her. She said they seemed very much in love and spent hours talking to each other on the sofa, all lovey-dovey, holding hands. Harrie was very prim about this sort of physical intimacy, any display of which she regarded as improper. Had Allen and I behaved like that, she would have been furious.

Certainly, while Jacqui and I were living in her house, the nearest we had been allowed to any boyfriend we brought home was nothing less than an armchair away. I am surprised Harrie was so tolerant towards John and Yoko, especially in view of their public honeymoon in bed, which must have shocked her.

In Ireland the only people who knew about my connection with John were Allen's family. They good-naturedly restrained themselves from too many comments on John and Yoko's behaviour, except for a well-loved granny who declared them to be off their bloody rockers. I agreed with her!

Ireland put a geographical distance between us. Before that we had been closer in land terms and also because he was with Cynthia, whom we knew. His relationship with Yoko took him into a different realm and I followed his media movements via television, like everyone else. Sometimes, even then, he seemed very close; at other times, a complete stranger. Sometimes I was glad no one knew of the relationship; sometimes I was sorry, because I felt very proud of him; at times I was embarrassed, at times amused. I was extremely happy with my anonymity when they were tied into bags and publicly in bed with the world's press (no matter what the reason!). Strolling naked through the clothes in Tommy Nutter's in Savile Row, looking for shirts, was crazy stuff for crazy people. But these crazy people were in the limelight. Who else would have been allowed to select clothes with such lack of panache anyway?

I learned all about John and Yoko's visit when I took my baby son Nicholas over to Liverpool later in the year to introduce him to all the family. Harrie gave me two silk blouses Yoko had inadvertently left behind. 'Go ahead and have them,' she said. 'I'm sure Yoko won't send for them.' They were a very small size eight and a tight fit even on me. It surprised me how tiny they were. I had seen photographs of Yoko, but hadn't realised that she was so petite.

Soon after that Allen and I decided to leave Belfast and move back to Liverpool. We found a flat in Hope Street opposite the Anglican cathedral and would have continued living there a while longer but for Mater, my aunt in Edinburgh, who came down to see us. Mater insisted that we ought to have a house now that my second baby was expected. It obviously made sense to take out a mortgage instead of paying rent and so she gave me a down payment to put on a house for my belated twenty-first birthday present.

We found a four-bedroom house in Wallasey, the less posh side of the Wirral, opposite where Cynthia and Julian were living. Much later, in 1975, when the eldest children were both at school, I went back to teaching at Caldy Grammar school. Allen was now in a wholesale food business and at last we were on our feet. It was good to be back in Merseyside again, among our old friends, and it meant I could get down to London to see Leila without too much trouble. She subsequently moved up to Manchester.

Leila, who now had three children, returned in 1968 from Germany where she had been working as a consultant. She was now practising as an anaesthetist at the Ear, Nose and Throat Hospital in Camden Town, North London. She moved into a Beatles flat in Sloane Street. We all went to stay there and I stayed for longer periods to help her with the children, having travelled initially from Belfast and now from Liverpool. The wardrobe in one of the bedrooms was stuffed full of Beatle suits, jackets, trousers, shoes, coats, etc, and I tried many of them on. They were there for the taking: David did have some. Whoever would have thought that the owner would no longer be here? There was never any sense of urgency about anything then. There was *always* time.

One day in 1969, I was strolling down Regent Street whilst Leila's children were still at school. It occurred to me that I was just around the corner from Savile Row where the Apple offices were. As I had never been there before, I decided to call in and see John. It was a very grand white building with a large reception area where a glamorous blonde was sitting behind an enormous desk. She smiled at me, very welcoming, as I approached. 'Is John in, please?' I asked.

The smile faded from her face. 'Yes, as a matter of fact he is,' she said, sounding several degrees less friendly than she had looked a few seconds before. 'And who are you?'

'Well, actually I'm his sister,' I told her, somewhat taken aback by the sudden inquisition. She looked slowly around the reception room, as if to make sure everyone was listening, and said very sarcastically, 'I'm *terribly* sorry, but John Lennon hasn't got any sisters.' 'No, of course not,' I rejoined, turned around and walked straight back out of the door. I didn't feel like fighting with anyone's secretary about whether or not John was really my brother. It was too stupid for words. When I told John later what had happened, he upbraided me for not insisting that somebody should at least let him know I was there. Better still, he said, I should have barged past her and walked right up the stairs to find him. Looking back, I suppose I should have been more assertive. The poor girl had probably heard the same line dozens of times. But I had been so astounded to hear that I didn't exist, I simply thought to myself, 'Oh, forget it'.

My cousin David had been to see John at Apple. As a man, he was an unlikely suspect as an hysterical Beatle fan. Leila, David's sister, had been there, too. It was also easier for her. She was ten years older than me and out of the fan age group. But a long-haired girl in her twenties like me looked like any one of the young women who devoted their life to hounding John. I never tried to go there again after that.

Leila was once invited, with Mimi, to a boardroom lunch at Apple. She, too, was very concerned about John's newly adopted lifestyle, as Harrie had been.

'To be honest, I didn't get much of a chance to talk to him,' she says. 'It was still early days in his courtship with Yoko and I couldn't get a word in edgeways between the two of them. I can tell you, though, he looked absolutely dreadful from that silly diet he was on and he appeared to be quite ill. To be truthful, I was shocked seeing him sitting there, hunched over his warmed-up lentils and a few ridiculous grains of rice.

'I remember someone bringing up the subject of their nude cover on the *Two Virgins* album and Mimi saying, "It would have been alright, but you're both so ugly. Why didn't you get somebody attractive on the cover, if you had got to have somebody naked."

'It *was* silly of them, wasn't it? It was really only childish exhibitionism. It was almost as if they said, "Well, we've done everything else, now what can we do? Right, that's it, we'll take our clothes off." It's what little children do at the beach.

'It's difficult to be plunged suddenly into fame like he was, but I had no time to be saying, "What *is* John doing? He's not eating properly. He shouldn't be behaving like that." I was busy doing night duty those days and I was always exhausted.

'Another time I went to see them both at Weybridge, and I did have a good old chat with John then. I think he and Yoko got married a few days later. That nasty little boy didn't even tell me about it. I should have boxed his ears.

'There wasn't much contact after that, except through the post. When my mother died later in 1973, he wrote to me and I know he felt guilt. You see, when his mother was killed I just dropped everything and ran to his side. But when Harrie was dying and he didn't come, believe me she felt it. It would have made her very happy to see him during those last few weeks. He apologised profusely on the phone some months later. He said he knew he should have taken the trouble to come.

'It was impossible for me to remain cross with John for too long, especially since he later admitted to having problems himself during that period, mostly with drink. That's really when he started writing home again, and he wrote semi regularly after that until he died.'

John's affection for Yoko overtook everything else. She seems to have absorbed him totally for a time. This greatly upset the other Beatles, especially when Yoko started taking part in their recording sessions. Wives and girlfriends had never been allowed to intrude into the hallowed domain of the studio. But John wanted Yoko with him all the time and everywhere. Before the Beatles had been a band of four, as close as brothers. Now they were four plus one and it wasn't working out.

Having been introduced to Yoko's weird and wonderful world of art, John wanted to broaden his scope. The limitations of working as a group with the Beatles were too restrictive. He wanted to branch out on his own and put the Beatles behind him. His work with Yoko, the only person he felt was in tune with him artistically, would now come first.

It was the end of 1969. It was clear that the Beatles were splitting up and the news came as a great shock, not just to all the fans around the world, but also to John's family. I personally wasn't particularly concerned. After all, it was John's life, his decision to strike out on his own, no business of mine. I was curious, of course, how it would turn out for him and where this new life would lead him. That I wanted him to be happy goes without saying.

John later explained the Beatles' break-up like this: 'The Beatles really collapsed after Brian Epstein died and we made *The Beatles* double album. If you took each track and compared them, it was just Paul and a backing group, George and a backing group, and me with a backing group. Although I personally rather enjoyed it at the time, that's really when we broke up.'

It was never up to me, or anyone else for that matter, to judge what John did or didn't do. I shared his idealism along with many others and understood how he felt about many of the causes he took up, although I wouldn't necessarily have reacted in the same way. Incredible as some of his and Yoko's schemes were, they were prompted by sincere beliefs. Certainly his efforts and commitment to world peace demanded respect despite some of the methods! John was a genuine man and a very moral one. He was motivated by good principles.

Through his songs John became a very powerful and well-known figure in the world. He often achieved more than many politicians did, but he never claimed to be more than he was – a man who made music and wrote songs and who had a deep concern for the liberty of man and was always ready to help the underdog. He had a deep respect for truth and, whatever he was doing, I feel that he would have never failed to be honest to himself. It may have been our upbringing – always being shielded from the truth by the family in case it hurt – that made him so determined to play things straight. John, Jacqui and I – we had all seen the damage that could be done when they weren't, however well intentioned the lie.

His honesty with himself was an integral part of his talent. 'My life is my art,' he once said.

He felt human existence was too important not to take seriously. 'If you're sitting on a beach and the water's up to your ankles, there will always be people to tell you, "It's too deep, the current is too strong, there are too many sharks." Well, it might be silly but I'm for just diving in and learning how to swim. It's really the only way.'

Bed-ins, bagism, nudism. Everyone began to wonder what John and Yoko would try next. John didn't care what anyone thought. He wanted them to sit up and take notice, and they did.

He said himself, 'All this rubbish Yoko and I get up to at least starts people off discussing the issues and seriously considering whether there just might be a better alternative to the way we're living.'

The older members of the family didn't discuss John's antics. As far as they were concerned, such activities were best not talked about. Even we younger ones were somewhat embarrassed that we might be associated in some way with John's extraordinary behaviour.

John himself started having second thoughts about his and Yoko's unconventional tactics to achieve publicity for their causes. 'I have to admit that some of my early political activities with Yoko were pretty naïve,' he said later. 'But Yoko was always political in an avant-garde kind of way. She had this idea that you must make use of newspaper publicity to get across the idea of peace. Any excuse, such as our wedding, was enough. She believed that you should try and make people laugh too. The trouble with Jerry Rubin and Aby Hoffman was that they never wanted laughter, they only wanted violence. I've never been into violence myself, although I'm aware sometimes of violence inside me. I have a violent nature. Like the song says, all you need is love. That's really my ultimate political belief. We all need more love. But I found that being political tended to interfere with my music. I'm still a musician first, not a politician. You see, I believe that music is not peripheral to society, but an absolute necessity.'

I know that one of my brother's greatest worries, which

exceeded even his political concerns, was his transatlantic split from his teenage son Julian.

Says Leila: 'I haven't really seen Julian since he was a baby, but I do know John always felt rather guilty about not being around very much as he was growing up.

'On several occasions John asked me to go and visit him, but I just thought, "What is Julian going to say?" An auntie he couldn't remember meeting suddenly coming into his life when he's almost fifteen wouldn't mean a thing to him. John should really have kept both Julian and Sean closer to his family than he did if he wanted us to visit them. He was very wrong to have neglected that side of things. Julian should have had the opportunity to get acquainted with his aunts and uncles and cousins. However, I don't think it would mean much to Julian now. From what I've been able to gather through the papers, he seems to be successful in his own right and good luck to him. I only hope he does well for himself. I'd really like to meet him eventually.'

Later on, John was concerned because Julian, who normally rang every week, hadn't been in touch for the last three. John was essentially a decent bloke and, because he was, his guilt about Julian crept up on him time and time again. In the old days, had Julian not made contact, John wouldn't have got into a tizzy. But on that occasion he asked me to find out what was happening to Julian. 'Can you go round and see him,' John asked. 'His mother must have a cob on.'

I didn't get around to it the first time he asked, and he kept on asking. He even sent me two letters about it, and that wasn't like the old John at all. The reason I was reluctant was that I hadn't seen Cynthia for a long time. Making contact with her again might be a little embarrassing. I had liked her, but I was his sister and she was his ex-wife, and we had naturally lost contact. Eventually, it was Allen who made me go, saying John had only asked this one favour. So I went round to Cynthia's house in Hoylake. Cynthia answered the door, obviously very surprised to see me and not a little embarrassed, as I was too after not seeing her for so long. We exchanged niceties, but she didn't appear to want to talk beyond that. I have a feeling she had friends there and didn't want to enter into complicated explanations by introducing her ex-sister-in-law. I asked if I could see Julian but she told me he was out. I left John's message for Julian with her, asking him to ring John at the Dakota Building in New York. Maybe we shall meet one day and we'll be able to chat about his father and grandmother together. That was the last I ever saw of Cynthia. I am certain she never did get over carrying a torch for John.

LEFT: John and Julian signing autographs at Kenwood, 1967

RIGHT: A family portrait of John, Cynthia and Julian taken by Ringo Starr

LEFT: Cynthia with Julian and schoolfriend

ABOVE: Jacqui and myself in Ireland, 1969.
John was sent a copy of this photograph in
1975, and it now sits amongst other family
photos on John's famous white piano in the
Dakota

RIGHT: I prefer this photograph of myself,
aged 21, to any other, because of the
striking resemblance I bear to our mother

John 'marrying' Georgie Fame and Carmen Jiminez at her 21st birthday party in 1967.
Ringo was dressed as an Arab, and Brian Epstein came as a clown

The Beatles pose together at John's palatial 72-acre estate, Tittenhurst Park, 1969: one of
their final photo sessions as a group

The Beatles join Maharishi Mahesh Yogi at a Meditation Centre in Bangor, North Wales, in the summer of 1967

LEFT: Paul appears minus his moustache at a gathering to mark the release of *Sgt. Pepper's Lonely Hearts Club Band* in 1967

RIGHT: At the first International Satellite telecast of *Our World*, 1967

Chapter Five

TEARFUL REUNION

'All my life I've wanted a real family and now I realise I've had one all along.'

JOHN in his first transatlantic conversation with JULIA

'I'm still me. You're still you. And all this "Big John Beatle" stuff is just bullshit.'

JOHN in a letter to his cousin LEILA

'I've been baking bread and looking after the baby. But everyone keeps on asking me "*what else*" I've been doing. To which I say, "Are you kidding?" Because baking bread and babies, as every housewife knows, are full time jobs! But as I watched the bread being eaten, I thought, "Hey! Don't I get a gold record or knighted or *nothin'*?"'

JOHN LENNON

For the first time in our lives John and I lost touch completely for over four years. I had married, had two children, done normal things, while John's life was even more turbulent than before. After the break-up of the Beatles he went off into seclusion for his primal therapy treatment and then flew off to America, never to set foot in his home country again. He could have been on another planet. All we knew about him was what we read in the newspapers. It seemed that his solo singing career, his trouble at home with Yoko and his Green Card problems were keeping him thoroughly preoccupied in New York. The realities of family and Merseyside were obviously far from his mind.

Despite the silence, he wasn't out of my thoughts. I knew he would come back to us and that he wasn't out of our lives for good. It happens like that in many families when a brother goes off to somewhere like Australia and gets so involved in his new life he forgets to write back home. You know you'll see him again one day. I could wait.

By 1975 my husband Allen and I were living in Wallasey on the Wirral. One evening Mater, my aunt in Scotland, telephoned to tell me she had a surprise for me. 'Do you want to speak to John, Ju?'

'John who?' I asked, any connection with my own brother not even entering my head. That shows just how long it had been. 'Brother John, *your* John,' said Mater impatiently. She went on to tell me that he was trying to get hold of 'the girls' and wanted her to let him know where Jacqui and I could be contacted.

'He says he wants to make everything up to you, Ju,' she told me.

I couldn't imagine what she meant by that. John had nothing to make up for. He was living his life and I was living mine. What else was there?

107

'He says he's been thinking a lot about your mother lately, and he wants to try and do something for you and Jacqui,' she said. I asked what sort of something he meant. 'John could easily help Allen with his business, you know. If you want anything, you mustn't be afraid to ask.' I was very happy that John wanted to make contact again. But I didn't need anything from him except his love. I had a husband with a secure job, who could look after me and our children. Had I ever been destitute, I doubtless would have tried to get in touch with him. I know he would have helped me without question. I did have a millionaire brother, after all. It would have been silly not to ask, had it been necessary. But that wasn't the case.

I have never really thought seriously about what it means to be a millionaire. I know what it is to be moneyless, to have enough money and to have money to spare, but not to have endless cash supplies. Sometimes I can quite easily consider myself to have unlimited funds, just because I have a regular salary supply, and can happily overspend on the strength of that idea. Then of course comes the reining in so that you can start all over again. Truly limitless financial horizons are not in my sphere. As far as John and his money were concerned, I never considered that he owed us anything, so when we did receive cash gifts, they were a complete surprise and welcome bonus.

Quite honestly, we probably would have been in touch long before had it not been for John's great wealth. The aura of fame and riches surrounding him sometimes made it difficult to maintain any sort of relationship at all. As far as I was concerned, his financial situation only served to keep him more out of reach of his family. It was like a barrier between the grandeur of his existence and our fairly mundane one in Liverpool. Moneywise, my brother was out there on the Milky Way compared to us.

Mater gave me John's telephone number in New York, 'the hotline', which I assumed went straight through to him in his apartment in the Dakota Building on Central Park West. She emphasised I mustn't pass it on to anyone, under any circumstances. As you can imagine John always did have a terrible time trying to keep his telephone number secret.

I put the number into my desk drawer and kept it there for

several days while I thought things over. I very much wanted to speak to John, yet I didn't want him thinking I was only ringing up because I wanted something. People were after John for things all the time, and he surely must have sometimes wondered if he was genuinely liked just for himself. I suppose it's a problem most ridiculously rich people have. Finally, I decided that John must know me well enough by now to know I wasn't like that. Five days later at midnight, which I reckoned was a reasonable time for John in New York, I dialled the number Mater had given me. I couldn't get through. There were strange noises on the line and an American girl's voice saying 'Hello', but that was all I got. So I tried again the following evening, and the same voice answered. 'Can I speak to John?' I asked. 'John who?' she said.

'John Lennon,' I told her, mystified why they didn't know who John was in his own home. 'Please tell him it's his sister from England.'

'And where did you get this number?' she demanded.

'From our aunt in Scotland,' I replied. There was a pause, then she told me to hold on.

She came back again with more questions. What was my married name? My maiden name? My father's name? It was getting ridiculous. She still wasn't satisfied when I told her. She asked me to hold on yet again. This time when she came back she wanted to know my father's middle name. 'Albert,' I almost shouted at her. It was too much for me. 'Really, let's forget it, I don't . . .', I had begun. Suddenly John's voice was on the line. 'Don't hang up,' he yelled. 'It's me! If only you knew how many sisters I had.'

It was like getting through to Henry VIII. 'No,' chuckled John. 'That would probably be easier.'

It was a wonderful reunion. That it was over the telephone didn't matter. The line was so clear he could have been back home in his native Merseyside, talking to me from the house next door. It didn't seem possible he was 6,000 miles away in another country, in a home I had never seen, in another sphere of life from me altogether. It was the most intimate conversation we had ever shared. Now, at twenty-eight, I was mature enough to have caught up with the seven years that divided us as children, and we could share our innermost feelings as we never had before. Different as our lives were, we were still the brother and sister we always had been and time had only changed our relationship for the better.

I said I had really missed him. 'Where have you been, John?' He was full of apologies for not being in touch. 'There really isn't any excuse, Ju,' he said. 'I'm sorry. We shouldn't have lost so much time together.'

I replied, 'That's all right. Come to tea and I'll make a jelly,' which was my way of saying there was nothing to forgive. He said he had been looking for Jacqui and me for months and thought of us regularly over the years, but hadn't known where to find us as we had both moved. He made the point that he'd been wrong, but so had we. He left various messages but somehow none of them got through until Mater's call. We all had different reasons for loving John. Quite apart from anything he became, he was always, as Leila says, one of the loveliest male members of the family. Don't forget we were top heavy with females, and I have to admit there was a little inter-family jealousy. The result was it took longer than it should have done for him to contact us.

After the initial hellos, his urgent need to get in touch soon became obvious. It was nothing to do with any wealth he possessed, nor the need to salve any conscience he might have by giving me a millionaire-style present, as Mater had suggested. He needed to talk about our mother, anything and everything we could bring to mind. Jacqui and I were the only two people in the world who could share his feelings about her in quite the same way, and that's why he had to find us. Only we three knew what it was like for us, as her children, not to have her any more. I couldn't ever have talked to Allen about her the way I did with John that night. The moments when it's good, a brother-sister relationship is a very tight bond.

For years I had found it virtually impossible even to mention my mother's name to anyone but Jacqui. The trauma of her death had affected me too deeply. I had learned to push the memory of it to the back of my mind, locked out from conscious thought where it hurt too much. Jacqui had been my only occasional release valve. John hadn't had a Jacqui or a me and he sought some relief through his course of primal therapy with American psychiatrist Arthur Janov, whose treatment aimed to free the subconscious of unhappy early experiences. Our telephone conversation unleashed a flood of memories and bottled-up emotion. It was very tearful. But it was also therapeutic and I felt that many emotional cobwebs had been blown away for both of us. After seventeen years, we were only just beginning to come to terms with her death. It opened a slow release valve for me.

Hearing the warmth and emotion of John's voice, I thought how lucky we were to have each other. He was a good person who cared about me and about how I felt, as much as I did about him. It was as if we had never been apart since that dreadful day when she died.

'It's such a bloody shame she isn't around,' said John, his voice angry through his tears. 'It still haunts me. There isn't a bloody day she doesn't cross my mind at least once. I *hate* her being dead.'

We didn't talk about his life in America at all. It wasn't that kind of factual I-did-this and I-did-that call. We talked about feelings and family, the things that matter most in anybody's life, whoever they are. John was rediscovering his family roots, I felt. He was a deeply decent man with traditional values about home and family. His creativity sought freedom through outrageous behaviour but his basic being was still that of the same solid citizen he always had been.

He asked me about Jacqui's little boy, John, and about my two, Nicky and Sara, and Allen whom he had never met. He said he wanted us to go to New York to see him. 'Please come soon. Just let me know when. We'll have to make some arrangements. I'd come to Liverpool if I could, but if I go they will never let me back in again. I'm stuck here until I get my Green Card.'

He wanted to know about our cousins Leila, David, Stan and Michael, his generation of the family. He asked me to tell them he would be in touch with them all very soon. It was as if the memories triggered off by all the talk about our mother had made him want to secure his future with the family he still had.

'Have you changed?' he asked. 'Have you still got long hair? Do your babies look Irish, or do they look like you?' He was fascinated that my oldest child Nicky had exactly the same beautiful auburn hair as our mother. He said he would love to see him. The conversation kept coming back to Mummy – we had always called her that, even John when he got to his teens, and we still did. He bet I missed her not being there now that I had children. I did then, and I do now. Almost more as time passes. She would have made them a wonderful grandmother, I know.

'God, I made a noisy house,' said John. 'How I'd have loved her to be around for the whole Beatle show.'

He was right there. She would have been overjoyed to see him make it. She would have loved all the razzmatazz, too, going to a Beatle première or watching the Queen pin an MBE on her son's chest. I'm not so sure, though, that she would have been as pleased about his giving it back in November 1969.

John reminded me about Mummy's favourite pink party dress, the one with gold and silver stars speckled on the skirt. 'She looked beautiful,' he said.

'Daddy always said she was the most beautiful woman in the world,' I told him, and explained how my father had kept that same dress hanging in his wardrobe for years afterwards. It had long stopped smelling of her perfume but it summed up her happy, bubbling personality for long after she was dead which was why he kept it. I would sit and stroke the material for hours. She was the most wonderful person. I told John that her friends in Liverpool still spoke about her all these years later. What a remarkable woman to be missed daily after so long. No wonder the son she had was John.

We were both still missing her very much, and talking about her so frankly was very upsetting. But it did us good getting the angry hang-ups off our chests, being able to laugh and cry at the same time as we remembered the fun moments too. We both agreed we still couldn't believe what had happened and it was a comfort in itself that we felt the same way. We got extremely weepy then.

John had heard about my father's death. 'I was really sad to hear about it. I was a thoughtless bastard not to come and see you and Jacqui,' he said. 'They've always written a lot of crap about him and me, but I was always very fond of him. You know that, Ju, don't you? But you've still got Nana, haven't you?'

'Nana' was what we called our grandma, my father's mother. I had to tell John that she, too, was dead.

'Christ. We seem to lose everybody, don't we?' he said.

He wanted to know everything about my own family and where we lived now. When I told him we had a house in Wallasey, on the east coast of the Wirral, he said, 'That's the scruffy side. You must move round to the posh bit.'

'Don't fancy it,' I replied. His next suggestion was for us to get a farm in North Wales where he had gone with me as a child to spend holidays in a cottage belonging to my father's Welsh relatives. John had always loved the country. He was crazy, too, about Scotland where he had spent summer time with Mater and Uncle Bert. Bert still owned the croft in the Highlands where he had been brought up. It was on the northern tip of Scotland in the village of Durness and facing the Atlantic Ocean. It is one of the most beautiful and deserted parts of Britain. John raved on about it so much that Paul McCartney bought a farm in Scotland, without ever having been there before. At one time a large estate came up for sale in Sutherland, one of Scotland's loveliest counties. My cousin David noticed it and he sent John the advertisement from *The Times* announcing the sale, half-joking, I think! I don't think John did anything about it as we never heard anything more.

But the idea of a Welsh farm definitely appealed to him.

'Go and look for one and I'll come and stay,' he said.

Well, I was quite happy where we were in Wallasey and there was plenty of room for him to come and stay, if he wanted. If he thought a farm was such a good idea, why didn't he buy me one?

'Don't be silly,' he replied. 'I haven't got any money. I'll buy you a company house.'

I suppose that the reason John's money was tied up with his and Yoko's company was for tax reasons, but an arrangement such as the one he was suggesting wouldn't have suited me at all. I was too independent a person to want any compromise. My home was for my children and had to belong to us, not to some company. In fact, neither of the two houses John got for members of the family were bought in their names. That was Mimi's house in Bournemouth, and the house John originally bought for Harrie, who looked after Jacqui and me in Woolton, and where Uncle Norman still lives. Who could say what might happen in the future? Allen and I needed more security for our family than that.

Our call went on for at least two hours. He wanted to speak to Jacqui and I promised to get her over to my house from Liverpool as she hadn't a phone herself. Still we talked. I didn't even think about the cost of the call until, right at the end, John suddenly remembered it was me who had rung him.

'When you ring again, call collect,' he told me.

'What do you mean, call Colette?' I asked, wondering who she was. I had little experience of America or American expressions.

'You know, silly, reverse the charges.'

'You speak English to me,' I ticked him off.

When the phone bill came in, it was enormous. I learned to call collect!

I thought about John a lot over the next few days. At the end of the week a letter arrived which meant he must have sat down to write it immediately. He went back over everything we had talked about on the phone and said it had brought so much back to him. Yoko had been to hospital again and he said he felt he was having 'the frigging baby' himself, and couldn't wait for the birth. 'Don't forget to tell Jacqui to ring,' he reminded me again, and then signed off, 'Yer brudder John, uncle to yer kids'. It was as if he wanted to assert his family connections by making sure that the niece and two nephews he had never seen at least knew about his proud status as an uncle. My children, too, were part of the roots John was seeking again. It was the first of many lovely letters from him after that, typed out on his IBM.

The letters that everyone received from John in the mid-seventies gave an account of his life and thoughts at the time. I'm sorry that I didn't treat mine more carefully – but some were thrown away as read and answered and others put in a drawer. I have moved house several times since then and have lost a Hornby train set as well as some of these letters! Leila kept hers together, intending to give them to her children as an insight into their cousin John (though eventually these were sold by her daughter). It may seem extraordinary, or at least puzzling to some that I didn't store them better, but it never occurred to me that the writer would no longer be there. I didn't think of them in the same light as the children's earliest doodles and scribbles which, like most mothers, I still keep. After all, they were simply personal little notes from my brother and not, as far as I was concerned, historic Beatle memorabilia or the inspired writings from the cultural leader of a generation which could have made thousands in Sotheby's.

After that initial call, John and I spoke at least once a month with either him calling me or me calling him 'collect'. The topic of conversation was always the same – the family and, most of all, Mummy. John talked and talked about her, reliving his child-hood. We both revelled in the memories, the happy days, the laughter, the idiotic humour, which always brought us back to the same point: the tragedy and absurdity of her death and our need of her. He repeatedly said how he missed her. He told me he was glad I was called Julia. My daughter would have been Julia too, but David adopted the name for his first daughter who was born the year before. John had Julian, too, so the name would always be carried on. It still upsets me, though, when I hear his song 'Julia' on the Beatles' *White Album*. It was released just after Allen and I got married, and it has very strong associations for me.

I miss Mummy even now, at forty years old, just as much as I did when I was twelve. Having your mother disappear from your life is shattering: the extremely bizarre way in which the family presented her death to Jacqui and me left a gaping hole that never quite heals up. Your emotions seem to be suspended in mid-air for the rest of your life. Sometimes I can get quite desperate for her and John must have felt the same. I think about her every day and I often find myself talking to her. Some people may think I am crazy or clinging or both, but the memory of her is still very much alive. If I have a problem, I find myself saying to her, 'Help, Mummy. What shall I do?'

John was very aware that the family he still had were alive and well and longing to see him. He talked about coming over to

England. He had made millions, but that didn't matter one iota. He wanted something that money couldn't buy: the comforting warmth of a large family surrounding him. 'I've been wanting a family, and I've had one all along,' he said.

'Well, we're all here,' I told him.

Much as he missed his family and Liverpool, John didn't want to come back to England permanently. He loved New York and he loved America and he wanted to stay there. 'It's a fantastic country,' he told me. 'When you come over, you'll see what I mean. It's all happening in America.'

As everyone knew, John was still trying to secure a Green Card to enable him to leave and re-enter the United States at will. 'I'm not leaving this damn country until I know I can get back in again,' he explained during one call. 'If I leave before I have the Green Card, they won't let me back. I'm trapped like a rat.' He had top lawyers working on his case and he was very upset it was being made so difficult for him, especially as he loved the country so much. He felt that the US Government didn't like him and were using what he called 'a couple of lousy grams of hash' as an excuse to boot him out of America.

I heard later that he believed his telephone was being tapped. Apparently, someone in New York had given him a special number to ring which, if it sounded engaged, proved the phone you were calling from was tapped. He had called that number from his apartment one day, and it *was* engaged. He naturally didn't announce his suspicions to me on the telephone. It made me wonder, if people were listening in, what they made of the calls between John and me.

When Sean was born on 9 October 1975 John was too busy playing Daddy to ring me and I didn't hear from him until several weeks later. I just hoped that the card I had sent him for his birthday had arrived in time. It had, on the same day as Sean was born, exactly 35 years after John's birth. When we finally spoke, he told me how overjoyed he was. He had made a conscious decision to take over the care of his son until he was five, while Yoko took charge of their office and conducted the family business. He said he loved having the baby and talked about Sean like a new mother.

John had reached an age when he realised the importance of a family. Sean was his immortality. With John to guide him through his early years, he would be a chip off the old block and the name of Lennon would survive. John was essentially a family man. He had been brought up in a close family atmosphere and showered with love from all sides. He had lost out once on having a family of his own, partly through his life as a Beatle, and he wanted to start again. He was indescribably thrilled at Sean's arrival. Sean was John's new life and I was delighted that despite the fame and fortune, John was achieving such happiness in his personal life through looking after Sean and enjoying his babyhood. He began to shake off the old public image which, at times, had almost been that of Public Enemy Number One.

He chattered on to me for hours about what it was like being a father again, a real one this time, he hoped. It was all proud talk about sleepless nights and feeding times, Sean's first smile and watching him grow. He was always patting himself on the back, telling me I'd no idea how worn out he was seeing to the baby.

'I've been there before,' I told him and we had a great laugh when he realised how over the top he was being. He loved walking Sean in his pram in Central Park and glowed with pride about his son. Because of touring with the Beatles, he had almost completely missed out on Julian's early years. This was a whole new experience and he didn't want to miss a single moment of Sean's development. He did everything for him; obviously all the things he had not been there to do for Julian.

He had refused to let Cynthia have a nanny for Julian. He maintained that the first five years of life were the most influential and that only a parent should be in charge at that important time. So John got Sean up in the mornings, dressed him and breakfasted him, gave him lunch and was always around the house ready to play with him. When he wasn't involved with Sean, he spent his time reading. Books were still his greatest passion. He hadn't read so much since he was a schoolboy, curled up on his bed in Mendips, engrossed in the fantasy worlds of *Gulliver's Travels* and *Alice in Wonderland*.

I think, with Sean, John wanted to do for that little fellow what he hadn't done for Julian. 'I completely screwed things up,' he told me one time. 'He's an amazing kid, though, in spite of what I did to him. Sean is going to get my attention from the word Go.'

Leila commented, in her typically forthright way: 'I hope John's going to give his new son a lot more than his money and his genes.'

John now had all the time in the world to give to Sean, but that only served to make him feel even more guilty about his treatment of Julian. He told me he was determined what had happened with Julian wasn't going to happen again. He threw himself completely into looking after Sean and devoted his time to him unconditionally. John was reborn as a family man through Sean. He was searching for an identity and he found it through that little boy. He began asking everyone for everything. Photos, family mementos, all the reminders of his childhood and his Liverpool background. He wanted the old family china Mimi had used at Mendips and a grandfather clock which had stood in the hall there. It had Uncle George's name inscribed across the face: George Toogood Smith. As children, we thought Uncle George's middle name was quite hilarious. Mimi packed up the china and the clock and sent them off to John in New York. This gathering of family mementos was for Sean's benefit, as an introduction to his family on the other side of the Atlantic. Having reaffirmed his own roots with the family he thought he had lost, John wanted to make quite certain that Sean was never in doubt about *his* heritage.

One night when John and I were on the phone, I told him I had just been looking at a beautiful picture of Mummy, pregnant with Jacqui, standing in Nanny's garden. Allen and I were both keen amateur photographers and we always did our printing at home. Allen had found this old negative of Mummy and blown it up to a 20 × 16 print. I had to admit to John that he had been in the photograph, but that I had cut him out because I just wanted the picture of Mummy. John wanted it immediately.

He *had* to have this picture, he said. What other pictures had I got? Could I please send them to him immediately?

When John went away to America, he had taken family photographs with him. I couldn't understand why he was so desperate to have even more. He said he had given them to various newspapers and magazines, and they had never been returned. In a rash moment of wanting him to see every single picture of Mummy and the rest of the family, I stripped much of our collection off the walls and sent them to him. Yoko sent me a letter of thanks on John's behalf.

With his introduction to domesticity, John ventured into the kitchen. Baking and cooking, something he had never done before, became one of the highlights of his new life. 'What do you do with your lamb?' he would ask me over the telephone. Clearly he'd abandoned his macrobiotic diet! We swopped cooking disasters and gossipped away about our culinary achievements like two dedicated housewives exchanging notes over the garden fence. John said he was a good gravy maker and passed on his tips. I can't remember what they were, but I do know I still cannot make delumped gravy. He recounted in detail how he had baked his first loaf of bread.

He was so pleased with the end result that he had even taken a photograph of it with his Polaroid. The only trouble was that when he came to cut it, he couldn't. The knife bent. I suggested Vitamin C tablets in the dough to cut out the rigours of kneading. I then told him of my first solo attempt at scones and how Allen and I ate granite-hard lumps, hysterical with laughter. None of us had ever cooked at home.

John invited me to go to America. 'You've got to come to New York,' he kept saying. 'You'll have to get to know it the way Yoko and I did, walking the streets. Walking is the only way to see New York.'

Somehow that trip never got off the ground. The children were at school and I was teaching, and the holidays always seemed to get tied up with visits to France or to the family in Ireland. Neither John nor I pursued it, although we both had it in mind. You could have asked John for anything, and it would have been yours. If I had been specific, had said, 'Can we come next month?', I'm sure that John would have immediately told me to contact his office and ask them to send the tickets. When I look back, I should have been more assertive. But Jacqui and I were both reticent by nature. We never pushed ourselves on anyone, which included John. It is something I now regret — not

119

instigating arrangements for such a trip. We thought then that there was plenty of time.

Although John had been an urban dweller most of his life, he nonetheless loved the country and its lifestyle. I suppose that being at one with Mother Earth was part of his basic attitude to life, the same as his feelings about self awareness, honesty, family ties and regard for those less fortunate.

He wanted to know everything about the time Allen and I had spent in Ireland. Which counties had we seen? What coastlines had we explored? What did we think of Mayo? And would we like an island there?

He actually had one. It was called Dornish and was off the west coast of Ireland. It had no water, no electricity, no place to stay and the last inhabitants had been a band of hippies. 'You have it, if you want,' said John. 'Go and stay there. Live wild.' When I mentioned the lack of water, all John said was, 'Drink beer instead.' What a madcap John was. It was him all over. Potty and impractical. He had accomplished what many people only think about – buying an island surrounded by wild seas, cut off. That in itself is fantastic. What a celebration! Again, we never went there and I read that Yoko sold it last year. What a pity!

Another of John's wild ideas was for me and Allen to emigrate to America. He was captivated by the States and he kept emphasising what a beautiful country it was. He told me about the farm he had bought in Virginia. 'It's the most fantastic place, Ju,' he said. 'It's so beautiful there, you won't believe it.'

Allen and I had vaguely toyed with the idea of emigrating to North America, but to Canada, not the States. The minute he heard that, John immediately said he could help. There would be no trouble with Allen finding a job. He could easily fix up something in Toronto through his own contacts. But that idea, like so many other ways we discussed of meeting up on the other side of the Atlantic, came to nothing. We all thought there was so much time to plan our lives together.

Even though we hadn't seen each other for so long, we always had lots to talk about. It was never anything sensational, and would have been very boring to anyone outside the family. One night I had a very bizarre story to tell John, beyond the normal chit chat. I, so often accused by John's staff of being a fake sister, had a fake brother to report.

His name was Tony. He was twenty-two and came from Cambridge and turned up on my doorstep one morning with the incredible news that he was my long-lost brother. His words were: 'This may come as a shock to you, but I am your brother.' He was a pale, gaunt-faced boy. I felt so sorry for him. He had been adopted in Liverpool and then taken south by his new parents. He was quite convinced that my mother had given birth to another child after John, and before I was born. He said he was two years older than me, five years younger than John, and he knew all our names, including my mother's. He was just a poor nut-case, a deluded victim of Beatlemania. But he kept coming back. Once he left a bunch of roses and a Beatle album on the doorstep. I eventually asked Allen to go and see him by himself and we never set eyes on him again after that!

At the time he called, I didn't know about the birth of my half-sister, Victoria, in 1945, the year Tony said he was born. Although Tony definitely hadn't been right, he had obviously researched! I remember telling Leila about this strange young man, who had even visited my mother's grave in Allerton Cemetery, something I cannot bring myself to do. She was unusually quiet and didn't pass any comment. Her silence struck me as odd. Was there a ring of truth in this? It was the first inkling I had that something might be amiss in my mother's life. But Leila never let on that she knew the secret of Victoria Elizabeth, my mother's wartime love-child. As the eldest cousin she had been party to the information, but had been sworn to secrecy by the Stanley sisters. Once again, it was the conspiracy of silence at work, as I realised later when I discovered the truth about Victoria for myself. It was years later, in about 1985, when I was talking to a publisher and he actually mentioned this baby. He could see I knew nothing about it. I was stunned. He told me to go and talk to Mimi. It was extremely embarrassing for both of us. It rang a bell with what Leila had touched on and I just knew it to be true, although it sounded and seemed ludicrous. I finally asked Nanny and she told me about it, albeit reluctantly. It was no good telling her we should have

121

known. The protection plan was at work again. So much began to make sense which had hitherto been nonsense.

In December 1976 John rang to wish us all a happy Christmas. I thought how nice it would be if I could give him a present, something he'd value for its thought. To go and buy something would be silly. What could I possibly afford that he didn't have ten of already?

It had to be a very special present, one that not even money could buy. Priceless in its own right. I gave it a lot of consideration, coming up with various ideas. Then it dawned on me. It had to be something I could make for him. It would be like when your children make you a birthday card, with all those loveable little squiggles, instead of giving you a shop-bought version. All I had to give John was my time. The effort of making it would represent what I wanted to say and give.

The girls in our family have always embroidered. My grandmother taught her daughters, and Mummy in turn had started to teach Jacqui and me. She only had time to teach us the simplest stitches, but she'd already set us on the road to knitting. She taught us all to knit, John included. We used to sit in the kitchen following her instructions as we learned to knit dishcloths with telegraph pole knitting needles and thick balls of string. After that, Harrie took over. We are both really rather good at embroidering now. A hand-embroidered tablecloth was the answer; a large one, as John surely had a large dining table in his Dakota apartment, sewn on the finest Irish linen. Whenever he used it for some marvellous meal he had perhaps cooked himself, maybe even my lamb recipe, he would think of home. The basic cloth I bought was almost the size of a bedcover. It was a painstaking exercise I planned. I intended to embroider the whole surface, some twenty-four square feet, so that it was completely embossed with stitches. I never did finish the cloth. I had already spent hundreds of hours working on it, and had still only covered a quarter of the surface, when suddenly John wasn't there any more to receive it. The cloth now lies in a chest of drawers. I might finish it one day, perhaps for my daughter Sara when she gets married. A gift of love for a special person.

Chapter Six

Ten Minutes Silence

'We have lost a genius of the spirit.'

NORMAN MAILER

'Our poor long lost little cousin. At work he was a Beatle but at home always, *always* a brother. Our dear Judy's finally got him back at last.'

LEILA

'First up John Lennon was always a good friend. He was never the abusive, aggressive guy some people made him out to be. When John was killed I think he was just hitting his peak, both as an artist and as a human being. And that's really the saddest thing of all isn't it? John's death.'

GERRY MARSDEN

'John loved and prayed for the human race. Please pray the same for him. Please remember that he had a deep faith and concern for life and, though he has now joined the greater force, he is still with us here. There will be no funeral. The silent vigil will take place December 14 at two pm for ten minutes.'

Yoko Ono Lennon

After eighteen months of telephone calls, John and I drifted away into our separate worlds again in the latter part of the Seventies. We were both to blame. We thought we had all the time in the world. As it turned out, I would never talk or write to him ever again.

We had built up a close affinity in those long talks about our mother, and we were closer than ever before. But our lives, although so entirely different, were keeping us both busy. John was fully involved with Sean in the cocoon he had built around himself in the Dakota. I had moved house twice and was working as a supply teacher as well as coping with my family commitments.

Besides, I wasn't always brave enough to face the barriers necessarily surrounding John. Ever since being put down by that secretary at the Apple office, I had been overcautious about approaching him. My run in with the telephonist at the Dakota almost put the lid on me ever ringing again. I kept reminding myself that he had to be protected from the oddest people who were always after him. His staff, after all, were only doing their job.

There was also another problem. Yoko was now being very protective. I rang him a few times and on each occasion I was put through to Yoko. I always rang late at night so that it would be a reasonable time for John in New York, not some ungodly hour that might have disturbed him. 'John's not available,' she'd say, giving me no explanation, or 'John's asleep.'

Well, it was midnight for me in Merseyside and I was certainly ready for sleep, but for John across the Atlantic it was six or seven o'clock in the evening. Sometimes I rang at three o'clock in the afternoon, New York time. A bit early for bedtime, or do they have siestas in New York? After that, I didn't ring any more.

'Don't think about it, lovey, do it,' was my mother's favourite maxim, and I am very sorry I didn't follow it. Sorry I didn't try a few more times to get him on the phone, sorry I didn't just pack up the children and head for New York as he so often suggested. Had I been more decisive, the children could have met their famous uncle. What fun it would have been for them, seeing the skyscrapers and getting to know John. I always made a point of talking about him to the children. I referred to him as Uncle John, never simply John, to establish the relationship with him. They knew his singing voice from records and they had seen him dozens of times on television. Nicky was already nine and Sara seven when I became pregnant with David. I told them how nice it would be for the new baby, having a much older brother and sister, and I made a comparison between me and Uncle John, saying what fun Jacqui and I had with him.

It's always easy on reflection to see what you should have done at the time. I am sorry I didn't persist, regret I took ages answering those lovely letters, one of which had begun, 'Dear Julia/allen et al in walla walla sea side.'

I know Leila felt the same. Although she and John weren't as close as they had been at the time of my mother's death, they still exchanged occasional letters and phone calls. She says, 'Looking back at things, I wish I hadn't been so busy that I didn't go and box his ears a few more times. On the other hand, though, there's the actual business of life to be got on with. But he did send me some lovely letters. They were just John being nice and normal, not the John who played silly jokes on the public. To me they showed his true nature, like the good lad he used to be.

'Unfortunately, some of those letters have been lost. Some, I have to admit, I actually threw away because he was going on about this man who read Tarot for him and I thought it was a lot of nonsense. Occasionally, he would send me one of the Tarot readings, all drawn out in his own hand. I'm sure Sotheby's would have loved them. But they still went in the bin. Of course, his naughty little Christmas cards couldn't ever be put up with the rest of the family's.

'I've recently had an argument with Yoko about some of those letters. My daughter felt she needed a little extra money at one point, and so she teased and nagged me until I finally gave in and let her put a few of them up for sale. I'm sure John wouldn't have cared a toss, but Yoko was really very rude about it.

'She rang me up one evening and really told me off about it. She implied that the publicity surrounding the letters might adversely affect a concert she was planning and that we were somehow trying to muscle in on her life. But none of us are interested in the limelight. We have our normal lives and our families which should be enough for anyone. Given the circumstances, I thought I was very pleasant about the whole thing. I simply said, "Look Yoko, John was our blood. You were only married to him, and a second wife at that." All things considered, I think that was a fair comment. However, she hit the roof and used some very nasty language. From then on she stopped sending the little Christmas gifts that John always insisted upon. I believe she even rang my brother David and told him she thought I should apologise. As far as I'm concerned, though, I have nothing to feel sorry about. She had no right to ring me up and criticise my morals.

'I would never *ever* seek to profit out of my relationship with John. When he was still alive I could have had what I liked for the asking, but I never even thought about it. I am a doctor, for pity's sake. My family has never gone without and never will if I can help it.'

The Christmas gifts Leila was talking about were the hampers John sent to everyone in the family. His office rang up Harrods or Fortnum & Mason and arranged to have them sent. They contained various Christmas foodstuffs like champagne, Stilton, pâté, smoked hams and plum pudding. They are still sent to most members of the family, but not Jacqui and me. Leila's hampers stopped for one year after that conversation, but then resumed. Jacqui and I were removed from the list without explanation, but it never bothered us.

The hampers were not very personal gifts, and although the contents were enjoyable, none of us ever felt desperately excited about them. I have known the non-drinkers of the family to donate bottles of the spirits to the milkman as a Christmas gift.

In the spring of 1980 Allen and I went to live in the walled city of Chester, on the Welsh border, about half an hour's drive from Liverpool. That autumn we had some great news from Leila who had managed to get through to John. She said that he had hinted he might be coming back to England the following January to promote his comeback album, *Double Fantasy*, which he and Yoko had made together. Sean was now five and at school, and John was now free to go back to work. He and Yoko spent August and September at the Hit Factory, the recording studios in Manhattan, working on twenty four tracks, fourteen of which were chosen for *Double Fantasy*: seven by John and seven by Yoko.

After virtually being a housebound recluse, tied up with domesticity for five years, John started giving interviews again to promote the album. It was horribly ironic that what he had to say on one occasion was almost an insight into the way the world would be talking about him just a few weeks later.

'Why were people angry at me for not working?' he said in that interview. 'You know, if I was dead, they wouldn't be angry at me. If I had conveniently died in the mid-Seventies, after my *Rock 'n' Roll* album or *Walls and Bridges*, they'd all be writing this worshipful stuff about what a great guy I was and all. But I *didn't* die, and it just infuriated people that I would live and just do what I wanted.

'I'm going to have fun with it now, like I did when we first started. I never could have written "Starting Over" in 1975. I am finding myself writing like I first used to write. These past five years have helped me liberate myself from my own intellect, and my own image of myself. So, I could write again without consciously thinking about it, which was a joy. This is like our first album. It's to say hi, hello, here we are. The next one will verify it, and then we'll start work on the third.

'It's fun to be rocking and rolling now, but if it gets not to be fun, then I'll just walk away. Because I know I *can* walk away now. The single is called "Starting Over", because that's exactly what I am doing. It took me forty years to finally grow up. I see things now that I never knew existed before.'

Despite John's optimism about the future, he must have been slightly nervous about the reaction to his first fully fledged artistic offering in five years. I kept abreast of his movements through the papers and everyone seemed genuinely pleased that he was back at work again. By late November *Double Fantasy* was climbing to the top of the charts on both sides of the Atlantic and his trip back to England was announced as definite.

Not since Beatle days had John given so many interviews and we saw him frequently on television. Once, on an *Old Grey Whistle Test* programme, he looked straight into the camera, winked and said, 'Hello to all the folks back in England.' We had known he meant us in Liverpool and now we couldn't wait for him to get back.

The ninth of December 1980 started off like any normal weekday morning, with the usual rush of getting the children off to school, feeding baby David, and doing a million things at once. It was a quarter to eight and Allen had already left for work in Liverpool. Nicky and Sara were getting themselves dressed, to a chorus of 'hurry-ups' from me, and David was in his high chair having the last mouthfuls of his breakfast spooned into him. I hadn't bothered to put on the radio for the news. There was too much bustle and clatter around the house without that blaring out and adding to the noise.

We didn't have a telephone, as when we moved in there wasn't one and we still hadn't got around to putting one in. We had only been there nine months and were still pulling walls down and putting in windows. Generally getting the house how we wanted it. For emergency use, I had already arranged with my neighbour Sylvia across the road to allow me to give her number to relatives and close friends.

When the front doorbell rang, I assumed it was the postman. But when I opened it, I found Sylvia. She said that Leila was on the telephone for me.

I dashed back into the kitchen, plucked David out of the high chair, tucked him under my arm, and then ran across the road to Sylvia's, feeling sick and desperately worried. If Leila was calling me at that hour, something was terribly wrong. It was like getting a black-edged telegram.

As soon as I picked up the receiver, Leila said, 'Have you heard the news? It's John. He's been shot.'

I can't remember what more Leila said, or even if she told me

129

that John was actually dead. She didn't have to. I knew he was. My memory of that morning is a haze after that. I was too devastated for anything to mean anything. I can't really remember, but I think Sylvia must have taken David off me. She didn't know my relationship with John but she realised the connection when she saw the look on my face as I gasped out John's name into the receiver. I know I was crying and crying. I couldn't believe it.

My mother, my father and now my brother. How many more great gaps did there have to be before my life became one big empty hole? No one seemed safe. There were no rules about anyone dying. The law of death had gone wild. It made me feel no one in the family was safe from it. My children suddenly became very vulnerable as well. For weeks afterwards I had terrible nightmares about them which woke me up screaming in horror. There was an accident black spot at the back of the house where a child had been killed a short time before we moved in, and I became obsessed with fear about it.

If anything were to happen to one of my children, that would be it. I wouldn't be able to take any more.

I can't remember what I said or did when I got back to the house from Sylvia's. I switched on to auto-pilot and somehow got the children off to school without them knowing. Afterwards I realised it had been thoughtless not to tell them, but I wasn't capable of rationalising. No one at school knew about their relationship with John and something might easily have been said about the murder, which would have been very upsetting for them.

My mind was numb. I sat in a daze waiting for Leila to come from Manchester where she worked in a hospital. She arrived about an hour later, and the only thing I remember about the rest of that day was that we cried for most of it.

Leila had to get back for her youngest son, Robert, who would soon be home from school. I sat in the kitchen, waiting for Nicky and Sara. I couldn't bring myself to turn on the radio. Leila had told me what she had heard and I didn't want to know any more. When the children came home, I sat them down and told them. What I said exactly or how they reacted, I cannot remember. It was part of the blank that day became. I only know I felt relieved as nothing had been said at school, and that I could tell them the right way. They watched the television, they were young enough to cope. I couldn't even bear to go into the room where the television set was, in case John's face came staring out at me from the screen. I put David to bed and, as soon as the other two children had gone, I went myself. It seemed the only place to go.

During that autumn I had said to myself dozens of times, 'If John doesn't make it in January, we'll definitely go to New York.' I was well aware we had lost time again and I had promised myself that I would push everything else aside and make the effort necessary to see him. It was ironic it had taken me so long to be that determined about going. It was just something I left too late.

For months afterwards I was haunted by the thought that our family was tainted by the aura of violent death. There is hardly a dead relative of mine who hasn't died in tragic circumstances. Even Harrie and Mater died from terrible illnesses. Mater died from cancer of the pancreas three months after it was diagnosed, and Harrie from a prolonged hepatitis. I desperately hope, though, that from now on everything is going to be all right. Last year Nicky went train spotting and fell backwards off a bridge on to a road twenty feet below. He could have been killed or chronically crippled for life. Sara rang me up at a friend's house where I was chatting over coffee and in a single breath told me, 'Mummy, Nicky's in hospital but it's alright, he's only broken his leg.' She is a very smart girl. She didn't give me time to get alarmed.

She hadn't got the damage right, but he was still incredibly lucky. He had a broken thigh and a broken wrist and in only six weeks was back on his feet.

I had not seen John for years, but when he died it was like having an arm cut off. I can't explain my feelings, even to myself. During the following week I still avoided the radio and the television, although I could manage newspapers. They weren't as emotionally demanding as a voice or a picture going over John's life or, even worse, a re-run of an interview with John talking on the radio or looking out from the television as if he was really still there. As for listening to any of his records, the thought made me wince with pain.

131

I never heard directly from New York. Yoko didn't ring, although quite honestly I never expected her to. Later on I picked up a newspaper and happened to see a statement she had made.

It said, 'I told Sean what happened. I showed him the picture of his father on the cover of the paper and explained the situation. I took Sean to the spot where John lay after he was shot. Sean wanted to know why the person shot John if he liked John. I explained that he was probably a confused person. Sean said we should find out if he was confused or if he really meant to kill John. I said that was up to the court. He asked what court – a tennis court or a basketball court? That's how Sean used to talk to his father. They were buddies. John would have been proud of Sean if he had heard this. Sean cried later. He also said, "Now daddy is part of God. I guess when you die you become much more bigger because you're part of everything." I don't have much more to add to Sean's statement. The silent vigil will take place on 14 December at 2 pm for ten minutes.'

The full horror of what had happened was just beginning to sink in when my friend Dot turned up to comfort me. Dot and I had met as neighbours in Wallasey. Although I was now in Chester and she had moved to Wales, we still kept very much in touch. As with all my friends, other than those who came from Liverpool and had grown up with John, Dot didn't know that John was my brother. She'd often heard me mention other people in the family – Mater said this or Harrie said that, or Mimi and Nanny are going to do this, that and the other. When she read in the newspapers about John's aunts and mother, at first she didn't connect this same catalogue of names with me. There was no particular reason for her to. Neither my name nor Jacqui's was mentioned, which was proof that our policy of keeping out of John's limelight had really been effective. Then Dot started thinking about it, and she said to her husband, 'If I didn't know any better, I'd say this was Julia's brother.' Finally, she realised it was too much of a coincidence and came from Wales to see me. When she saw the state I was in, she didn't even have to ask.

I shall always be grateful to Dot for her attention and affection at such a time. She even cut all the clippings from the newspapers about John's death, not just the one paper she normally took but from all the others, too, knowing that I wouldn't want to read them until later.

I didn't in fact read them for a long time although I am glad I have them now. Deep down, I didn't want to know about it. Besides, it was too much of a trauma reading what everyone else felt about John's death, while I was still struggling with my own feelings.

Within hours of John's death, both Paul McCartney and George Harrison issued press statements.

George's read: 'After all we went through together I had, and still have, great love and respect for him. I am shocked and stunned. To rob life is the ultimate robbery. This perpetual encroachment on other people's space is taken to the limit with the use of a gun. It is an outrage that people can take other people's lives when they obviously haven't got their own in order.'

Paul's read: 'John was a great man who will be sadly missed by the world, but remembered for his unique contribution to art, music and world peace.'

Everyone wanted to know everything about John from the lips of those who had been closest to him. Mimi and Cynthia were in the front firing line and they were pursued relentlessly by the press. The whole family was obviously overcome by grief, and it must have been supremely difficult for Mimi and Cynthia to cope with their emotions as well as all that aggravation. It was undoubtedly hard for Cynthia, who was still mourning her love for John. At least that, too, could now be put to rest.

Finally, they both agreed to talk about John. The world was so anxious to hear what they felt, they would never have been left in peace until they did.

'Since his mother died John always looked upon me as his mother,' said Mimi. 'There was never any possibility that he would be just an ordinary person. He'd have been successful in anything he did. He was always just as happy as the day was long. I will never recover.'

Cynthia, in an emotionally guarded statement, said, 'Despite the fact that we were divorced, I continue to hold John in the highest regard. I would like to talk to you about John but I know that, if I tried, the words wouldn't come out. It is very, very painful. All I can do is to stay here in England and try and keep my mind off it.'

There was no funeral, just the silent vigil. No one from the family went except for Julian. He was the only person whom Yoko personally invited. As for myself, I simply didn't want to go, and the rest of the family may well have had their own reasons for not going. I hadn't seen my mother or my father buried, and being at the vigil for John would have been to have all three die at once. Inevitably, there have been people who have asked what I feel about the man who killed my brother. He was a very confused and sick man and he obviously needed help. It was desperately sad that his mind had got into such a state it could dictate such an action. By taking John's life, he has almost taken away his own.

I felt desperately sorry for Sean. John devoted so much time to him, making his mark on him as a loving father. He must miss his daddy dreadfully. Two sons lost John, Julian in babyhood because the Beatles were always touring, and Sean just as he must have been learning what a wonderful and special father he was.

In 1985, five years after John's death, Leila decided to write to Sean. She was worried about his losing contact with his roots on this side of the Atlantic. We had heard nothing about him, although we knew he was aware of us. Sean had been the reason John had asked for all the family mementos from his Liverpool childhood and the pictures of our mother. Leila knew that John, with his great sense of family values, would have wanted us to keep the lifeline open between Sean and his Merseyside inheritance. What prompted Leila to write initially was a television special about John's life to commemorate the fifth anniversary of his death. The film enraged us all and we were deeply insulted the way our family had been portrayed. I rang up the director and told him so.

Our mother came over in the film as an empty-headed nitwit from a Liverpool slum who abandoned her child. John was presented as an unloved orphan-like figure, not as the man he really was who came from a large and very loving family. Nothing was right. Even the beautiful Cynthia was shown as a scruffy woman in a headscarf.

One of the salient reasons for finally deciding to write this book was that I wanted to try and set the record straight about our family, especially about our mother, as John wasn't there to do it. Had John been alive now, there would have been no need. Since his death there have been so many unfair and malicious comments about her in the press, I felt I had to do something. They were mainly concerned – as in this film – with John being allegedly 'abandoned' by Julia. John would have said, 'Don't read it.' Maybe you can, for the most part, get above it all when you are rich and famous, but it's more difficult for me. After all, it is *my* mother we are talking about as well. I have my own children to think about, and I have to consider their views about the grandmother they never saw.

We were very concerned that Sean might be getting the wrong impression about his father's family. It was, after all, an integral part of Sean's own existence. Yoko had appeared with him at the end of the film to make her tribute to John, and it is unlikely that she would have appeared in the film without approving it first.

It was well before Leila's run-in with Yoko over John's letters and, at this time, although her relationship with Yoko wasn't close by any means, it was still viable. So she wrote Sean a series of letters, telling him everything she could about his grandmother Julia and the rest of the family.

'Yoko was always very good about sending little Christmas gifts to the family here in Britain,' says Leila. 'So, therefore, I didn't really feel I was too much out of place writing to Sean about his grandmother. I think I ended up writing him about four letters. Unfortunately, there was absolutely no reply. My theory is that he never even got them. Personally, I think there's somebody in New York that might just as soon be happier if Sean didn't really know about his father's family. If that's so, then all right. There's nothing more I can do about it anyway. To each his own, I say.'

Sean is twelve now and it would be marvellous if he could come to Liverpool and see for himself how his father's memory lives on in his adored home city. The sadness is that John left without knowing he would never have another chance to say goodbye to it.

Wherever you go in Liverpool, there's a reminder of John and the group he made into history. Shops and restaurants named after the Beatles and their songs, the Abbey Road pub, the John Lennon Memorial Club, windowfuls of Beatles souvenirs with John's face grinning out from the T-shirts, a lifesize statue of Eleanor Rigby sitting on a bench, waiting, as the fans sit beside her having their picture taken, and all those parts of Liverpool like Penny Lane and Strawberry Fields which are living Beatle history.

I went back to Penny Lane recently, and found Mr Leong's, the Chinese laundry our mother used, still there. I could still remember Jacqui and me standing there, sniffing like the Bisto kids from the gravy advertisement as the compelling odour of sweet, warm, clean washing wafted up our noses. His is one of the few original shop fronts left in that legendary Liverpool street, really quite nondescript despite its romantic connections. At the far end is a row of ordinary red brick houses, a community centre and a sports ground, where the most eventful happening the day I went was an amateur football match. At the top end, where Beatles coach tours stop to let the tourists off, you have no problems knowing where you are. It's Penny Lane everywhere. Penny Lane Record Shop. Penny Lane Accommodation Bureau. Penny Lane Bakery. And, quite naturally, The World Famous Penny Lane Wine Bar (home-made minestrone, chicken and mushroom pies and sandwiches). Until the Beatles, no one thought of naming *anything* after Penny Lane. It was just another one of Liverpool's unusually named streets like Buttercup Way and Zig Zag Road. On and off for many years, Penny Lane was left without a street sign. Souvenir hunters kept stealing the plaque from the wall. Now Merseyside Council have solved the problem by placing a new sign high up on a wall, well out of reach.

In October 1986 I went shopping in the Cavern Walks Centre where a statue of the Beatles playing their guitars dominates the main plaza. To my amazement, the plinth that day was covered with a mass of flowers, from simple bunches to magnificent bouquets. Then I remembered. It was 9 October. John's birthday.

There were cards signed by people from all over the world. 'We miss you, John', 'We'll never forget you', 'In memory of a great man'.

These constant reminders of John are still painful for me, although it is easier now than it was. The reason I never went into Beatle City was that I couldn't bear the sadness that it makes me feel. Beatle City, the world's only permanent exhibition of Beatles memorabilia, was housed in a yellow submarine structure which had portholes for windows. It is closed temporarily, while they move it from its present site on Steel Street to a permanent exhibition centre being opened in an exciting new development in the Albert Docks, on the Mersey waterfront.

Obviously I know Liverpool extremely well and I have often taken my foreign language students on Liverpool city tours. Beatle City was always on the itinerary. I never went in myself but waited for them in the café area, outside the main exhibition hall.

I already knew Ron Jones, then the manager of Beatle City. One day, as I was waiting for my students, he came up and said he wanted to ask me a favour. He had a group of Americans coming to Liverpool for a Beatle tour, and would I drop in and just say hello to them? I was a little sceptical, but was persuaded to do that for him.

On the appointed evening I arrived at the Atlantic Tower Hotel and met Ron in the bar, as we had arranged. But where were the Americans? Ron had a surprise. The handful of people I thought I was going to meet for a little chat over a quiet drink had become a full-scale audience who were now lined up on rows of chairs in the hotel conference room, waiting to applaud my entrance. I nearly collapsed with fright.

In fact, that evening was such a success, I willingly did it again when Ron asked me the next time. They were charming people. There were about a hundred, and they came from all age groups and all walks of life – attorneys, accountants, teachers, students, advertising executives, housewives. When I first walked on to the platform (pushed on to it by Ron might be more accurate), their faces were a blur. I hadn't got my glasses on. I fumbled in my bag, found them, and slipped them on my nose. When I looked up, I saw that several of them were crying. The sight of me in my

137

granny specs, looking so much like John, had quite overwhelmed them. I pointed out that they were on the National Health and worn by thousands over here!!

They had been to Hamburg and London, and the visit to Liverpool was the highlight of their tour. They couldn't have been a more mixed group, yet one common factor united them like one huge family – their unreserved hero worship for John Lennon. For the next hour, I talked non-stop answering their questions. They wanted to know everything about him. I thought it would be difficult, but they wanted to know such simple things on the whole. What did he eat for breakfast? What age did he start going out with girls? Was he expelled from school? Did he paint a lot? Did I think he had an American accent? What were our age differences? They kept telling me how wonderful it was to meet me, and they all wanted to take photographs, with me and them in the same picture. They were terrific people. Warm and friendly.

They made me realise what a tremendous place John had in so many people's hearts, and how broad his spectrum of appeal was. There was only one hiccup. A young man at the back, who Ron said was a law student, kept insisting I tell him what he called 'the truth about John and Paul's relationship'. He asked me at least three times. Each occasion I told him that I couldn't comment about the relationship between two people I had not been with at the time. Still he persisted. 'I am going to ask you one more time,' he shouted out rudely. I looked down my spectacles at him with my best schoolmarm glower, and told him, 'You're not in law school now. I said no!'

His interruption did nothing to spoil the warmth of that wonderful evening. I was very touched by those lovely people and I felt extremely proud that it was my brother who had generated all that feeling in them. It also made me very sad. What a waste!

John died on the verge of a new wave of talent and his genius was cut off in its prime. Those last records he made were wonderful – 'Woman', 'Watching the Wheels', 'Starting Over'. Many people thought that they were better songs than he had ever written before.

The birth of Sean resurrected John's confidence in himself as a human being. The five years he spent with him as a full-time father gave him the breathing space he needed to regenerate his talent. He had also needed that time to mature, for he was hardly out of adolescence before he was flung headlong into the inordinate success of Beatlemania. An art student at seventeen, a father at twenty-one, a world famous star at twenty-three. He hadn't had time to catch his breath, let alone mature at his own pace. He was forty when he died.

He re-emerged from his time alone with Sean as a new man, a mature genius relaunching his talents. He always wanted to be a writer, and I am sure he would have been, a serious one, too. The storehouse of his talent was hardly yet tapped, before the absurdity of his death.

JOHN LENNON'S FAMILY TREE

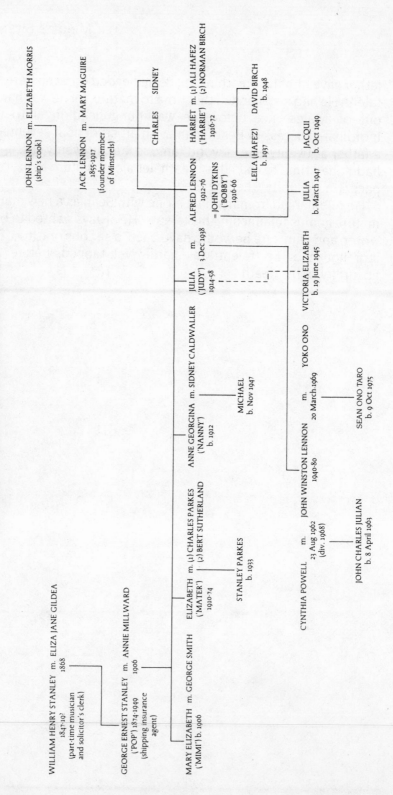

A Lennon Chronology

COMPILED BY GEOFFREY GIULIANO

26 *October* 1855.   John Lennon Sr, John's paternal grandfather (known throughout his life as 'Jack'), is born in Liverpool. He later became a founding member of the famous American travelling musical troupe, 'The Kentucky Minstrels'.

22 *August* 1874.   George Ernest Stanley, stern patriarch of John's mother's family, is born at 120 Salisbury Street in Everton. He spent many years at sea, later coming ashore to work as an insurance investigator for the Liverpool Salvage Company.

14 *December* 1912.   Alfred ('Alf') Lennon, John's seafaring father, is born at 27 Copperfield Street, Toxteth Park, Liverpool. His mother, Mary Maguire, was to bear two more sons, Charles and Stanley.

12 *March* 1914.   Julia Stanley, mother to John Lennon, Victoria Stanley, Julia and Jacqui Dykins, is born in Liverpool to Annie Millward and George Stanley.

1916.   John Albert Dykins, Julia's common-law husband and the father of their two girls, Julia and Jacqui, is born.

August 1917.   John Lennon Sr dies of a liver disease at the age of sixty-one, thus leaving his three sons in the custodial care of Liverpool's Bluecoat Orphanage.

18 *February* 1933.   Yoko Ono is born into the family of a wealthy Tokyo banker.

3 *December* 1938.   Despite strong objections from the Stanleys, Alf Lennon marries the free-spirited young Julia at the Liverpool Register Office. Immediately after the austere civil ceremony, each of them returns to their own home. Three days later Lennon signs on for a three-month tour of duty aboard a cargo ship bound for the West Indies.

10 *September* 1939.   John's first wife, Cynthia Powell, is born in Blackpool.

23 *June* 1940.   Stuart Sutcliffe is born in Edinburgh.

7 *July* 1940.   Richard ('Ringo') Starkey is born to parents Richard and Elsie at 24 Admiral Grove, the Dingle, Liverpool.

9 *October* 1940.   John Winston Lennon enters this world during a German air-raid over Liverpool at 7 o'clock in the morning. Shortly after his birth he is placed under his mother's sturdy iron bed at the Liverpool Maternity Hospital. He is called John after his grandfather and Winston in honour of the Prime Minister, Winston Churchill. Once again his father Alf is away at sea.

24 *November* 1941.   Randolph Peter Best, the Beatles' first really professional drummer, is born in Madras, India.

18 *June* 1942.   James Paul McCartney is born to Mary Patricia Mohin and James McCartney in Liverpool.

1942.   Finally giving in to family pressure, Julia Lennon reluctantly agrees temporarily to turn over care of her infant son to her sister Mimi and Mimi's husband, gentleman dairy farmer George Smith.

1942.   Despairing of her globe-trotting husband, Alf, ever settling down, Julia finally ends their 'on-again off-again' relationship. She is soon to meet and fall in love with congenial barman John Albert Dykins. Together they take a small flat in the then tatty Gateacre district of Liverpool.

25 *February* 1943.   George Harold Harrison, the youngest child of Harry and Louise Harrison, is born at 12 Arold Grove, Wavertree, Liverpool.

19 *June* 1945.   Julia gives birth to her second child, Victoria Elizabeth, at the Salvation Army's Elmswood Infirmary in North Mossley Hill Road, Liverpool. The father is not listed on the birth certificate but was thought to be an army gunnery officer. The infant girl was subsequently adopted and is believed to have been taken by her new parents to Norway where today her ultimate fate still remains a mystery.

September 1945.   Young John begins attending school at Dovedale Primary just around the corner from his aunt Mimi's home at 251 Menlove Avenue in Woolton.

July 1946.   Alf returns from sea unexpectedly and convinces Mimi to allow John to accompany him on an impromptu holiday trek to Blackpool, secretly intending to spirit the boy away to a new life together in New Zealand. Luckily Julia locates the two and takes John back home to Liverpool.

5 *March* 1947.   Julia Dykins, John Lennon's second sister and the first child of Julia and John Dykins, is born in Liverpool.

26 *October* 1949.   Jacqui Gertrude Dykins is born in Liverpool.

September 1950.   Young John Lennon is awarded a beginner's swimming certificate by the Liverpool Association of School-masters.

July 1952.   John leaves Dovedale Primary.

September 1952.   John starts at Quarry Bank High School for Boys.

145

5 *June* 1955.   George Smith, Mimi's husband, dies unexpectedly of an undisclosed liver ailment at home, aged 52.

15 *June* 1956.   Paul McCartney meets John Lennon for the first time at a Saturday afternoon performance by Lennon's schoolboy skiffle group, the Quarrymen, at St Paul's Parish Fête in Woolton. Shortly afterwards he is invited to join the group by Pete Shotton, a mutual friend of John and Paul (as well as being the Quarrymen's erstwhile washtub player).

September 1957.   Cynthia Powell, aged 18, enrols as a lettering student at the Liverpool Junior Art School. She soon transfers to Liverpool Art College where she first meets her future husband, fellow student John Lennon.

6 *February* 1958.   Crackerjack guitarist George Harrison joins the Quarrymen. The nucleus of what would later be known as the Beatles is now formed.

Spring 1958.   His Holiness the Maharishi Mahesh Yogi arrives in Hawaii to begin propagating his Transcendental Meditation Movement in the West.

15 *July* 1958.   Julia Lennon, John's mother, is knocked down and killed by an off-duty police officer suspected of drinking, just outside Mimi's home on Menlove Avenue. John and his sisters are at home with John Dykins, playing outside. Julia's final words to Mimi just before the accident were, 'Don't worry.'

December 1958.   John and Paul perform a few gigs together as The Nurk Twins.

29 *August* 1959.   The Quarrymen are invited to play at the opening-night party of the Casbah, a teenage coffee club run by Mona Best, Pete's fun-loving mother.

15 *November* 1959.   Now renamed Johnny and the Moondogs, the band fails an audition for Carrol Levis at the Manchester Hippodrome.

5 May 1960.   The flagging group, renamed once again as the Silver Beatles, fails another big audition to back singer Billy Fury. They are, however, chosen to tour with another young crooner, Johnny Gentle, on an upcoming trek through Scotland.

August 1960.   Paul McCartney invites Pete Best to join the Beatles as their regular drummer on their first trip to Germany.

Autumn 1960.   The Beatles make their first professional recording with members of their rival Liverpool group, Rory Storm and the Hurricanes, at Akustik Studios in Hamburg.

5 December 1960.   The Beatles' trek to Germany is interrupted after George is found to be under age by German immigration officials and is unceremoniously deported. The other Beatles soon follow and end up back in Liverpool, feeling beaten and dejected.

21 March 1961.   The Beatles appear at the Cavern for the very first time. Over the next two years they will play there 292 times.

1 October 1961.   John and Paul take off on a two-week hitch-hiking trip to Paris.

9 November 1961.   Wealthy Liverpool record-retailer Brian Epstein unexpectedly drops in to the Cavern to hear the Beatles after being deluged with requests for their first official record release, 'My Bonnie' (a German Polydor import).

3 December 1961.   Epstein invites the group to his office to discuss the possibility of taking them over as their manager. They readily agree.

1 January 1962.   The Beatles travel down to London to audition for Decca Records. Despite a rousing performance by the Fabs they were ultimately turned down by Decca bigwig Dick Rowe,

who ironically told Brian that 'groups with guitars are on the way out'.

10 *April* 1962.   Stuart Sutcliffe tragically dies of a brain haemorrhage in Hamburg. He was just 21 years old.

9 *May* 1962.   The Beatles are offered a recording contract with Parlophone Records, a tiny offshoot of the vast EMI entertainment empire. Their recording manager is the brilliant George Martin.

16 *August* 1962.   For reasons that remain a mystery even to this day, drummer Pete Best is unceremoniously sacked from the group and Ringo Starr is quickly brought in to fill the gap.

23 *August* 1962.   John Lennon marries Cynthia Powell in a civil ceremony at the Mount Pleasant Register Office in Liverpool. Fellow Beatles Harrison and McCartney attend.

5 *October* 1962.   The single 'Love Me Do' is released.

31 *December* 1962.   The Beatles make their final club appearance in Hamburg.

2 *March* 1963.   'Please Please Me' hits the coveted number one position on the *Melody Maker* chart.

8 *April* 1963.   John Charles Julian Lennon is born to John and Cynthia at 6.50 am at Sefton General Hospital in Liverpool.

8 *August* 1963.   Yoko Ono gives birth to her first child, daughter Kyoko. The father is avant-garde film-maker, Anthony Cox.

1 *February* 1964.   'I Want To Hold Your Hand' is the number one record in America.

9 *February* 1964.   The Beatles appear on *The Ed Sullivan Show* in New York. During their performance an estimated 73 million

television viewers experience John, Paul, George and Ringo for the very first time. Across America not a single solitary crime is committed by a teenager.

23 *March* 1964.   John Lennon's first book, *In His Own Write*, is published. Almost overnight it becomes an international bestseller.

10 *July* 1964.   A civic reception is held in Liverpool to honour its most famous sons; over 100,000 people attend. Among them are John's sisters Julia and Jacqui as well as most of Lennon's family.

15 *February* 1965.   John Lennon finally passes his driving test (after driving illegally for years).

12 *June* 1965.   Buckingham Palace announces that the Beatles will be awarded MBEs later that year.

24 *June* 1965.   John's second book, A *Spaniard in the Works*, is published.

3 *August* 1965.   John buys his aunt Mimi a lovely seaside bungalow in Poole, Dorset.

31 *December* 1965.   Alf Lennon suddenly reappears on the scene, this time to release his one and only record, 'That's My Life (My Love and My Home)'. Although initially it receives quite a lot of airplay it is critically panned and sells poorly.

4 *March* 1966.   John makes his infamous remark about the Beatles being more popular than Jesus Christ during an interview with British journalist and Beatle crony, Maureen Cleave.

31 *July* 1966.   Radio stations across America join together in an ad hoc ban on Beatle music as a direct result of John's controversial remarks on the decline of Christianity in the

West. Over the next few weeks there are reports of record burnings and other protests by groups ranging from the Ku Klux Klan to the Daughters of the American Revolution. In the midst of this furore John is persuaded by Brian Epstein publicly to recant his remarks in an effort to calm middle America's shattered faith in the Fabs.

29 *August* 1966.   The Beatles give their final American concert at Candlestick Park in San Francisco.

9 *November* 1966.   John meets Yoko Ono for the first time at a special preview showing of her one-woman conceptual art show, 'Unfinished Paintings and Objects', at the Indica Gallery in London.

26 *May* 1967.   *Sgt Pepper's Lonely Hearts Club Band* is released just in time to kick off the infamous 'summer of love'.

24 *August* 1967.   The Beatles and an entourage of girlfriends, wives and hangers-on attend an introductory lecture on Transcendental Meditation given by the Maharishi at the Hilton Hotel, London.

27 *August* 1967.   While attending a special weekend meditation seminar held in Bangor, Wales, the Beatles receive word that Brian Epstein has been found dead in his London townhouse due to an unexplained overdose of drugs. The Maharishi attempts to comfort them by reminding them to try and 'be happy' and 'don't worry'.

5 *January* 1968.   Alf Lennon and his 19-year-old fiancée Pauline Jones meet John to seek his blessing for their forthcoming marriage. John is not too happy about this unexpected romance but reluctantly gives the two of them his support.

16 *February* 1968.   John, Cynthia, George and his wife Pattie join the Maharishi in Rishikesh, India, for an intensive two-month

instructor's course in transcendental meditation. The rest of the Beatles' entourage arrives four days later.

12 *April 1968.*   The Beatles leave the peaceful mountain ashram two weeks ahead of schedule after a nasty rumour circulates that the giggly Indian fakir attempted to compromise the virtue of fellow meditator Mia Farrow.

22 *August 1968.*   Cynthia Lennon sues John for divorce, citing his alleged adultery with Yoko Ono as the cause.

18 *October 1968.*   John and Yoko are busted for possessing 219 grains of hashish at their flat at 34 Montagu Square, London. A charge of obstructing justice is also brought against the couple who, according to old Liverpool chum Pete Shotton, had been warned of the impending bust beforehand.

25 *October 1968.*   Word leaks to the press that Yoko is pregnant. John Lennon is reportedly the father.

8 *November 1968.*   Cynthia Lennon is granted a divorce from John in an uncontested suit brought before magistrates in London.

21 *November 1968.*   Yoko suffers her first painful miscarriage. John remains constantly at her bedside at Queen Charlotte's Hospital in London, where he beds down next to her in a sleeping-bag for several days.

28 *November 1968.*   John pleads guilty to unauthorised possession of cannabis at Marylebone Magistrates Court. A fine of £150 is imposed as well as court costs of 20 guineas. The obstruction of justice charges are dropped against both him and Yoko.

29 *November 1968.*   John and Yoko's infamous *Unfinished Music Number One: Two Virgins* is released. The scandalous album cover depicts the free-spirited couple naked.

30 *January* 1969.   The Beatles play their last live public performance ever on the rooftop at Apple Studios. The impromptu gig
is filmed for inclusion in the Beatles' eclectic cinematic
swansong *Let It Be*.

2 *February* 1969.   Yoko Ono is granted a divorce from her former
husband, Anthony Cox.

20 *March* 1969.   John and Yoko are married in a quiet civil
ceremony on the island of Gibraltar.

26 *May* 1969.   The Lennons fly to Montreal to hold an eight-day
'Bed-In' for peace at the Queen Elizabeth Hotel. While there
they record the now-famous counter-culture anthem 'Give
Peace a Chance'.

1 *July* 1969.   While visiting John's aunt Mater in Durness,
Sutherland, Scotland, the Lennons and their children Julian
and Kyoko are involved in a car accident in Golspie. Although
no one is seriously injured John requires seventeen stitches
on his face and head. His son Julian is also treated for shock.

12 *October* 1969.   Yoko miscarries yet another baby. This time,
however, the pregnancy is sufficiently long for the child, a little
boy, to be given the name John Ono Lennon; he is buried in a
tiny white coffin somewhere outside London. Only John and
Yoko attend the service.

10 *April* 1970.   Paul McCartney publicly quits the Beatles.

31 *December* 1970.   Paul brings suit against the other Beatles in
an effort legally to dissolve the group.

3 *September* 1971.   John and Yoko say goodbye to England for
ever and fly off to America to make their new home.

16 *March* 1972.   The Lennons are served with a deportation
notice from American immigration officials due to John's 1968
drug conviction in England.

18 *September* 1973.   John and Yoko go their separate ways, John to Los Angeles while Yoko stays ensconced in their palatial seven-room Manhattan apartment. The couple have now been married for four years.

January 1975.   John returns home to New York and is reunited with Yoko. 'The separation just didn't work out,' he tells the press.

19 *June* 1975.   John files suit against former Attorney-General John Mitchell for what his lawyers call 'improper selective prosecution' relating to the government's deportation proceedings.

23 *September* 1975.   As Yoko is now pregnant once again, immigration officials temporarily halt their deportation proceedings against John on what they call 'humanitarian grounds'.

7 *October* 1975.   The New York Supreme Court reverses the deportation order against Lennon by a two-to-one vote.

9 *October* 1975.   Yoko gives birth to the Lennons' only child together, a 7-pound baby boy they name Sean Ono Taro Lennon.

5 *January* 1976.   The Beatles' former road manager and friend, Mal Evans, is shot dead by police in Los Angeles following an incident whereby Evans allegedly pointed a gun at officers responding to a domestic disturbance call. John is said to be deeply disturbed by the tragedy.

1 *April* 1976.   Alf Lennon dies of cancer at Brighton General Hospital. He was aged 63.

27 *July* 1976.   John finally receives his 'Green Card' at an immigration hearing in New York. John's only comment to the press was, 'It's great to be legal again.'

153

9 *October* 1976. John's self-imposed 'retirement' from show business and so-called 'house-husband' period commences. 'From now on,' Lennon tells the press, 'my chief responsibility is to my family.'

15 *October* 1979. John and Yoko contribute $1000 to the New York City Police Department for the purchase of several bullet-proof vests for officers.

14 *July* 1980. John and Sean set sail on the 63-foot sloop *Isis*, bound for Bermuda and accompanied by a five-man crew. It is during this holiday that John finally begins composing once again.

4 *August* 1980. John and Yoko begin recording at the Hit Factory in New York for the first time in six years. The music culled from those sessions is later to form the albums *Double Fantasy* and *Milk and Honey*.

9 *October* 1980. John celebrates his 40th birthday with his son Sean, who is five on the same day.

17 *November* 1980. *Double Fantasy* is released worldwide.

5 *December* 1980. John and Yoko are interviewed on their 'comeback' by *Rolling Stone* in New York.

8 *December* 1980. In the late afternoon, on his way out of the Dakota Building in Manhattan, John Lennon stops to give an autograph to a young man from Hawaii named Mark David Chapman. The two are photographed together. At 10.49 pm Chapman steps out of the shadows and guns down John Ono Winston Lennon as he returns home from a recording session accompanied by his wife Yoko. The world mourns John's loss.

Acknowledgements

The authors wish to thank the following people for their kind assistance and encouragement in the production of this book:

Apple Corps Ltd
Nicholas, Sara and David Baird
The staff of Beatle City
Val Bellis
Pete Best
Ray Beynon
Norman Birch
Debra Lynn Black
The Bull Brothers
Stefano Castino
Ray Coleman
Collins Publishers (Canada)
Jose and Christine Damiaiou
Dot Doyle
Dr H. Braden Fitz-Gerald
David Germain
Brenda Giuliano
George and Olivia Harrison
Leila Harvey
Trudi and Andy Hayden
William Hushion
Penelope Isaac
Joe Jelly
Richard Johnson

Ron and Dave Jones
Sheila Jones and all at MPL
Myrna Juliana
Susan Muirsmith Kent
Alcides Antino King
Leif and Lia Leavesley
Jill Kathleen Lee and family
Cynthia Lennon
Tanya Long
Allan Lysaght
Paul McCartney
Sri Chaitanya Mahaprabhu
Mangal Maharaj
Ward Mohrfeld
Carl Newman
The Betsy Nolan Group
Stanley Parkes
Charles F. Rosnay
Dimo Safari
Juliet Scott
Sesa, Devin and Avalon
Mr Singh
Skyboot Productions
Wendell and Gina Smith
Ann and Clare Starkey

3

ACKNOWLEDGEMENTS

Mr and Mrs Starkey
Ringo Starr
The Lucinda Vardey Agency
Tamra Williams

Georgie Woods
Bob Wooler
Tom Wronski
Dr Ronald Zuker

And a very special thanks to Carolyn Brunton without whom...

156